"Please Don't Kiss Me
at the Bus Stop!"

"Please Don't Kiss Me at the Bus Stop!"

Over 700 Things Parents Do That Drive Their Kids Crazy

Merry Bloch Jones

Andrews McMeel Publishing

Kansas City

Library of Congress Cataloging-in-Publication Data

Jones, Merry Bloch.
    Please don't kiss me at the bus stop! : over 700 things parents do that drive
    their kids crazy / Merry Bloch Jones.
        p. cm.
    ISBN: 0-8362-3589-4 (pbk. : alk. paper)
    1. Parent and child—Humor.   2. Parents—Humor.   I. Title.
PN6231.P2J66 1997
306.874—dc21   97-1219
                                                                                      CIP

Design by Mauna Eichner
Illustrations by Tanya Maiboroda

Attention: Schools and Businesses

Andrews McMeel books are available at quantity discounts with bulk purchase for educational, business, or sales promotional use. For information, please write to Special Sales Department, Andrews McMeel Publishing, 4520 Main Street, Kansas City, Missouri 64111.

To Robin, Baille, and Neely,
with kisses

Contents

Acknowledgments

Many thanks to all the young people who contributed their comments to this book, and to their parents who good-naturedly took those comments in stride. Thanks, also, to editors Chris Schillig, Nora Donaghy, and Jean Zevnik; agents Connie Clausen and Stedman Mays; Lynne Brunell, Lanie Zera, Susan Stone, Sue Small, Nancy Delman, Jane Braun, Ruth Waldfogel, and Michael and Jan Molinaro; Mrs. Bard's entirely excellent and articulate fifth grade class of '97 at Gladwyne School; my mom Judy Bloch and my late dad Herman Bloch for their insights and expectations; my sister Janet Martin and my late brother Aaron Bloch for shaping my concept of childhood; Baille and

Neely, two devoted research assistants, for bringing me all the joy any mother could hope for, and my best friend and husband, Robin, for his understanding, patience, and gentle endurance.

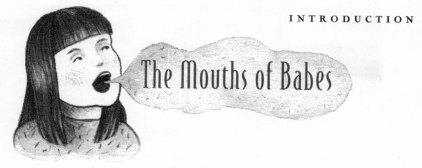

The Mouths of Babes

"It's so hard to get out the front door when you have a mother like mine."

It was more with resignation than indignation that my seven-year-old daughter muttered this complaint to her companion. I'd just chased after her with a jacket, insisting that she put it on before playing outside. From my child's point of view, Mother was an inconvenience, an obstacle to freedom. A person who blocked her way.

I'd expected my parenting to be better appreciated. But, once again, I was reminded that children have their own opinions and perspectives, and that mine are no exceptions.

In fact, my children made their opinions and perspectives clear from the moments they were born and continued to express them as they began to talk and move around on their own. They had tempers and often disagreed with me about what they could or couldn't eat, suck, spill, bite, pinch, pull, kick, throw, climb, cut, tear, touch, put on, take off, bring in, take out, dig into, or color onto.

But as I listened to my daughter's assessment of life with her mother at the front door, I realized, once and for all, that this flesh of my flesh, child of my body had her own eyes, own mind, own opinions, own world view, and—worst of all—her own image of me.

The implications were staggering. It followed that nothing her parents said or did was beyond criticism. Loving remarks, fond gestures, well-intentioned advice, gently imposed discipline, preciously held traditions—every element of our relationship would be examined and evaluated by her cool, assessing, alien eyes. Nothing in our lives would be too private for scrutiny, nothing too sacred for scorn.

It also occurred to me that my daughter might not

be alone in her attitude; other kids must regard their parents similarly. Driven for moral support, I investigated this possibility. I talked to children, teenagers, and young adults, and compiled their comments about their parents; the results make up the body of this book.

Their collective portrait of parents is at once amusing, embarrassing, poignant, and penetrating. With uncompromising realism and unblinking eyes, they reveal parents' faults, foibles, characters, and charms. With unwavering voices, they describe the affections and affectations, humor and humanity of what goes on behind America's closed doors.

The young people who contributed come from primarily non-dysfunctional, middle- and upper-middle-income families. They're located all over the country, representing all races and many religions. Their parents are, for the most part, college educated, employed, and happily married, although some are no longer married to each other. Interviewees are old enough to articulate their ideas (not younger than six) but young enough to remain economically and emotionally dependent on Mom and Dad (under twenty-one).

Kids came to me through their parents, families, and friends; I talked to them at playgrounds, parties, pools, schools, homes; in person, in writing, by e-mail, by phone. My daughters, husband, family, and friends assisted. Before I knew it, over five hundred young people had shared their honest impressions of their parents. Their comments, although not always flattering, can't be entirely surprising to anyone who has ever had parents themselves. Who among us, after all, has not had their buttons pushed when Mom or Dad gives advice without being asked or asks indirect questions instead of assertively stating an opinion? Or suggests a better way to do something and is invariably, annoyingly right?

As we get older, though, we begin to treasure—or at least to accept—these parent/child collisions. Instead of mere annoyances, they appear to be measures of intimacy, inevitable stumblings-into-each-other that occur when we awkwardly try to follow our parents' footsteps.

Accordingly, parents who read this book shouldn't be discouraged when they recognize themselves mercilessly portrayed in its pages; rather, they should realize that the comments reflect their children's natural passages to adulthood. As they mature, children have to separate from Mom and Dad. After all, only if they distance themselves enough to see parents objectively can kids follow their parents' leads while making their own choices and echo their parents' words while using their own voices.

Which is why, leaving my mom's house recently, I had to smile when she stopped me at the door. "It's getting cold out, Dear," she insisted. "You'd better take a jacket."

Total Embarrassment

Living with parents isn't easy. Even the coolest Moms and Dads can, at times, cause kids to cringe. And as children become teens and teens become young adults, familial cohabitation doesn't grow easier.

"*Everything* my parents do is embarrassing," states twelve-year-old Rachel. "Basically, I try not to be seen with them."

Certainly, not all children are so easily humiliated. Many patiently endure their parents, comforted by the fact that they are not alone; almost all kids are subjected to similar plights. Their parents are persistently, pathetically, and mortifyingly off the mark. Despite these assessments, though, parents do not lack influence.

Some young people, in fact, admit that their parents' attitudes and behaviors define and determine their own; whatever their parents think of as "cool" must, undoubtedly, be *not*.

"They mean well," sums up ten-year-old Jessica. "But they're clueless. What do you expect? They can't help it; they're just *parents*."

✣

My mom kisses me goodbye at the school bus.
Diego, 9, Brooklyn, N.Y.

✣

They think parents should be open and talk about everything with their kids. This means that they want to have discussions about whatever's embarrassing. Dating. Sex, AIDS, drugs. Venereal disease. My dad did a whole lecture about *crabs! Crabs!* The worst. Totally.
Anne, 13, Providence, R.I.

My mom's *pregnant*. It's, like, they have *sex*.
And everybody knows—*everybody*.
Norm, 12, Elgin, Ill.

They hold hands in public. And sometimes, they *kiss*.
Cody, 7, Upper Montclair, N.J.

They call me "Bubbles." In public.
Alan, 16, Pittsburgh, Pa.

Right in front of other people they call me "Cookie"
or "Muffin." Or "Noodle." Or "Doodlebug!"
Audrey, 7, Devon, Pa.

I'm "Sport." As in, "How ya doin', Sport?" or,
"How ya hittin' 'em, Sport?"
Ron, 14, Lexington, Ky.

&

My father calls me Yiddish nicknames with Russian
diminutives. "Sheyna Bananchek."
"Donutchka Kraseevaya."
Donna, 12, New York, N.Y.

&

I'm six-foot-three. Mom's five-foot-one.
She introduces me to her friends by saying,
"This is my baby."
Brad, 18, Seattle, Wash.

I'll finally get my hair just right. Smooth, so nothing
sticks up. And my dad'll walk by and tousle it. Then I
either have to leave it all messed up or make a big deal
about fixing it, as if I care about my hair.

Adam, 10, Boston, Mass.

❧

They shout, "Love you, Denny!" whenever I leave
the house, no matter who's with me.
For the next four hours, the guys keep at it.
They go, "Love you, Denny!"

Denny, 12, Chattanooga, Tenn.

❧

Mom goes outside in her nightgown.
Hair all pinned up. She stands in the yard, talks to
neighbors, the mailman. Whoever.

Pete, 14, Peoria, Ill.

"What's on your cheek? A pimple?" My mother
actually *said* that. With *people* around.

Kerrie, 11, Colorado Springs, Colo.

≪

Dad wears bikini bathing suits. Outside, at the pool.
With his belly hanging over the top.

Shawna, 11, Indianapolis, Ind.

Dad's a hotdog on the diving board
at the swim club. He challenges everyone to,
like, cannonball contests.
Brendan, 9, Baltimore, Md.

My mom's the librarian at my school.
She's, like, there. At my school. Every day.
When she sees me, she says, "Hi!" and waves.
Chris, 11, Merion, Pa.

When my mom sees my boyfriend, she says,
"Oh, hi, SweetiePie," and talks all
cutesy to him, like he's five years old.
Susanna, 13, Skokie, Ill.

Total
Embarrassment

13

My mom talks baby talk to the dog. "Aw, you such a
pwitty widdle poochy. Poochy wuv Mama?"
Lance, 11, New York, N.Y.

❦

They wear cologne. Both of them. I mean, you can
smell them coming. You know when they're home.
You know what rooms they've been in recently,
like, in the last three days.
JoEllen, 15, Tulsa, Okla.

❦

Mom talks in singsong whenever she talks to kids.
Like she's reciting nursery rhymes.
Paula, 8, Tacoma, Wash.

My dad pats the heads of kids he doesn't even know.
Marta, 10, Gladwyne, Pa.

❧

My mother's favorite subject is the size of my feet.
"Look at those feet! Can you believe it?
They're bigger than his father's! Most shoes
aren't even *made* in his size." I'm like, "Mom?
Can we talk about something else?"
Greg, 12, Memphis, Tenn.

❧

They love to tell people all the stuff I did when I was
little. How many times I slammed my hand in the car
door, how many stitches I needed. How I walked out
of the house and into the street in my sleep.
How I had diarrhea in an airplane so bad that it went
right through my clothes and into the seat.
Curt, 13, Raleigh, N.C.

Total
Embarrassment

15

My mom nudges me to point out boys she thinks are
cute. "Psst. Two o'clock—check it out."
Karen, 11, West Palm Beach, Fla.

⚭

My dad wears shorts with wingtips and black socks.
That's his standard, basic, warm-weather uniform.
What's up with *that*?
Ginger, 13, Buffalo, N.Y.

⚭

Dad'll wear Madras shorts with a Hawaiian print shirt.
He thinks its okay. If you say, "Dad, what're you
wearing?" he'll say, "It's summer." Like that's an
answer. Or he'll be completely baffled. He'll look
down at his clothes and say,
"What do you mean? What's wrong?"
Brenda, 14, Baltimore, Md.

Dad's the scoutmaster for my brother's troop.
He actually wears his scoutmaster uniform
to pick me up at school.
Vanessa, 15, Beaver Dam, Wis.

❧

When he's waiting for something, like for my sister to
come out of the locker room, my dad *dances* and *sings*.
In the *hall* at *school*. Once I told him this embarrassed
me, and he looked hurt, like he might cry.
Erica, 11, Santa Clara, Calif.

❧

My mom makes up her own songs. The words don't
rhyme and there's no real tune. She just sings.
Tracey, 9, Boca Raton, Fla.

They think everything I do is newsworthy. Headlines in the paper: "Jeffrey almost comes in third at the swim meet." Or, "Jeffrey misses getting an A in math by three points!" Or, "Jeffrey gets a haircut!" Like people need to know this stuff—it's all they talk about.

Jeffrey, 15, Ardmore, Pa.

❧

They talk about me to their friends. Right in front of me, as if I can't understand English. "Look how *tall* he is—can you believe it?" Or, "He's president of his class! He's the politician in the family."

Scott, 11, Deerfield, Ill.

❧

"Please Don't Kiss Me at the Bus Stop!"

They discuss me with people right in front of me. Like I'm not there. They say, "She's younger than she looks. She's only ten. She *looks* fourteen, doesn't she? But she *acts* ten. On her good days."

Amy, 10, Chevy Chase, Md.

Whenever we see relatives, Mom and Dad have to
discuss which part of my face looks like who,
whether my nose came from my aunt or my uncle.
Why I'm tall. Who I'm as tall as. Whose jaw I've got.

Paul, 13, Stamford, Conn.

❦

Whenever company comes over,
they want me to play my violin for them.
I don't know who hates this more,
me or the company.

Sue, 11, Rochester, N.Y.

❦

My mom *still* makes me go into the
ladies' room with her.

Alan, 6, St. Louis, Mo.

They don't get it. Especially my mom. She asked my friend if he wanted a wienie for lunch. "Would you like ketchup or mustard on your wienie?" I thought, let me die, right here, right now. Just let me die.

Steven, 10, Scottsdale, Ariz.

❧

If we eat out, they taste everybody's food. Pass forks around, stick a wad of eggplant parmesan in your mouth, cut off a slab of your flounder. Just once, I'd like to eat a dessert all by myself.

Alec, 16, Bethesda, Md.

❧

My folks eat like they're in one of those county fairs. Like they'll get points if they eat the most the fastest.

Carly, 17, Beaumont, Tex.

One of them will hum some oldie,
then the other one joins in and suddenly they're
doing this Motown thing, gestures and steps and all.
It's not so bad when it's in, say, the kitchen.
But they'll do it anywhere—
parking lots, supermarkets, malls.
Robin, 15, Sacramento, Calif.

Daddy growls at the dog. Snarls at him.
Grrrr.
Gabrielle, 6, Atlanta, Ga.

Dad shows off when he drives, rides bumpers, flashes
his lights. Passes people, gives them the finger.
Steve, 15, Irvine, Calif.

My parents obey speed limits. They never go above
them. My dad actually drives below the limit. People
pass us, honking and cursing.
Roy, 14, Yuma, Ariz.

I took a date to a party. We were driving
home when, all of a sudden, the car behind us starts
honking, flashing its high beams, weaving back and
forth. They pull up beside us. Who else?
"Hi, Mom. Hi, Dad. Meet Lisa."
Gib, 17, Manchester, N.H.

❧

Dad wears a rug. And I mean, a *bad* one.
Monica, 18, Minneapolis, Minn.

❧

My mom's hair is like, orangish-purple. She won't
admit she dyes it. She swears it's natural, and brags that
she doesn't have a single grey hair.
Tara, 19, Scarsdale, N.Y.

My mom can lose it right in public. Like, if someone butts in front of her at the bakery, she'll tell them about it. "EXCUSE ME! I *believe* I was here first." And that's just the *start*. She doesn't hold back her feelings.

Victor, 9, St. Louis, Mo.

❧

Our house is the bad pun capitol of the world.
Don't offer my father ketchup. He'll say,
"No way. I'm too fast for you." If a dog barks,
he'll say, "Dachsundheit!" Nothing's too stupid.
My cousin told Dad he got a parakeet. Dad asked,
"Why'd you get two? Isn't one keet enough?"

Lisa, 13, New Haven, Conn.

❧

When they have company, they like us to come in and say "goodnight" to everyone. In our pajamas.

Cynthia, 12, Pittsburgh, Pa.

When we have company, my father's
always the one to talk the most.
And he tells the same stories, again and again.
Morgan, 9, Syracuse, N.Y.

❧

My mom dropped my birthday cake at my party. Well,
she caught it as it slid across the backs of three kids.
They had blue icing all over their clothes, in their hair.
Blue icing was everywhere. Then she served the part
she caught. She laughed, thought it was a riot.
Kim, 10, Wynnewood, Pa.

❧

When Dad blows his nose, people probably hear it in
the next county. I bet it sets off burglar alarms down
the street. I half expect geese to land in the backyard.
Danielle, 15, Boise, Idaho

Dad likes practical jokes. Like, he'll reach out to shake
a kid's hand, and when the kid goes to take it,
Dad pulls his hand away. The kid's standing there with
his hand out, feeling like a dope. Dad offers the kid his
hand again. The kid can't believe he'd do it again,
so he reaches out to shake. This can go on for a while.
Dwayne, 12, Macon, Ga.

∽

When my dad yawns, the whole neighborhood
can hear it. It's a Tarzan thing.
Dahlia, 10, Norfolk, Va.

∽

Everything I do, they tell me it's good.
Good folding. Good trying. Good finding.
Good thinking. Good breathing.
Luke, 9, Boston, Mass.

They cheer for me. I was in the choir at school,
and we were performing, filing onto the stage.
When I walked out, they stood up and hooted.
All the other parents were quiet. Same with graduation,
school plays. Anything, any opportunity. I swear,
if they were around when my teacher took attendance,
they'd stomp and holler when she called my name.

Lynne, 14, Bala Cynwyd, Pa.

❧

My mom won't let me wear makeup. But she walks
around looking like that Tammy Faye Bakker.

Myra, 15, Ft. Worth, Tex.

❧

They dress alike. Color-coordinated outfits,
or unisex. Please.

Andrea, 14, Atlanta, Ga.

My mom wears T-shirts that tell you her mood
that day. "Hot stuff," or "Warning: PMS."
Lauren, 16, Orlando, Fla.

❧

Every Saturday afternoon, at about four o'clock,
they "take a nap" and lock their door.
It is *so* embarrassing. I go upstairs and turn on
the radio. I want to leave town.
Maggie, 15, Dayton, Ohio

❧

They smooch and cuddle. I have to leave the room.
Tim, 11, Conshohocken, Pa.

❧

They whisper to each other and giggle.
Like, what's going on?
Mike, 9, Grand Rapids, Mich.

They *love* to get dressed up. Decked out.
Like Fred Astaire and Ginger Rogers.
They act all elegant, puttin' on the Ritz,
Prince and Princess of the Bronx.
Paul, 15, Bronx, N.Y.

☙

They call each other pet names.
Beefcakes. Lambchop. I'm serious.
Will, 13, Memphis, Tenn.

☙

Mom talks to me about stuff like yeast infections.
Or body waxing. I have to close my eyes and wait for
it to be over. My dad thinks I'm still six,
wants me to watch Looney Tunes with him.
Ginnie, 11, Brooklyn, N.Y.

Total
Embarrassment
29

My mom announces to anyone within hearing range
that, oh gosh, she hasn't shaved her legs in weeks,
or that she has terrible cramps. Or that my dad
has been awfully horny lately.

Julie, 12, Charlotte, N.C.

❧

My mom told my swim coach that I couldn't swim
because I had my *period*. And *then* she wouldn't
let me quit—she actually made me go *back* the next
week as if nothing had happened.

Natalie, 12, Baltimore, Md.

❧

They gave my brother and me a whole lecture
about sex. Orgasms, pregnancy. Even AIDS and
how it spreads. It was *amazing*. I mean,
I didn't realize they *knew* about all that stuff.

Matt, 13, Albuquerque, N.Mex.

My mom decided I should use tampons. She drew pictures, stuck one into her fist to show me what to do. Then she handed me a box of them and stood outside the bathroom door, shouting instructions. She even offered to do it *for* me, and I told her, no way, that I simply could not deal with this. She said, "That's okay, Sweetie. We'll try again next month." I can hardly wait.

Lisa, 14, Denver, Colo.

❧

Out of the blue one day they handed me a pack of condoms. Dad winked. "Keep them in your wallet." Mom said, "We know you won't *need* them, Honey. But just in case."

Jake, 16, New Orleans, La.

Us and Them

Most kids make sincere efforts to be kind. They spare their parents' feelings by enduring public displays of affection, even tolerating tales of Santa Claus and the Tooth Fairy. Despite their best efforts, though, many admit that Mom and Dad sometimes stretch their patience by being predictably inconsistent, persistently uncompromising, strictly simple, or simply strict.

"I never get credit for the zillions of times I do things *their* way," complains sixteen-year-old Ted. "But, just *once* let them catch me doing what *I* want, and I'm grounded."

Regardless of the inequities, by the time they've

learned to talk, most kids have figured out their parents, adjusted to their eccentricities, tested their tempers, compensated for their limitations, and thoroughly mastered the arts of parental manipulation.

"If I keep my room clean," one savvy ten-year-old says, "my mom's happy. Then I can get away with just about anything."

❦

My mom always says, "You can never have
too many pencils or too much ginger ale in the house."
This is her tenet for life.
Ike, 18, Yonkers, N.Y.

❦

I'll be watching television, and my dad'll come in and
change the channel, right in the middle of a show.
Like, hello? I live here, too!
Nan, 9, Urbana, Ill.

My parents somehow can never put pencils away,
never set them down anywhere where you might expect
to see a pencil. If you want to write something down,
you need to search the house. Look under the
bookshelf, behind the stove.
Graham, 17, Darien, Conn.

They have 90,000 pens in the house,
and not one of them works.
Linda, 19, Fresno, Calif.

If my mom's cold, I have to wear a jacket.
If my dad's tired, I have to go to bed.
Sandie, 8, Austin, Tex.

My mom's always hot. I can see my breath
and she's turning the heat down.
Nate, 16, Evanston, Ill.

❧

Why is it that if my dad breaks a dish or my mom
spills an entire pitcher of lemonade, it's no big deal?
If *I* get a drop of ketchup on the floor,
it's an indictable offense.
Regina, 16, Tallahassee, Fla.

❧

I'm not supposed to disturb my dad when he's
"thinking." You know he's thinking because
he rubs his nose and responds to nothing.
Josh, 9, Richmond, Va.

They're always thinking. "Quiet," Dad says. "I'm thinking." They're quiet for, like, hours, staring at a table or a plant. If you ask, "Mom, what're you doing?" she says, "Just thinking." They think and think and think. Who knows about what? If you ask them for something, they'll say, "We'll think about it."
Jake, 9, Sacramento, Calif.

Dad reads my sister and me bedtime stories. He reads about three pages. Then he's asleep. Snoring away. Then Mom puts *him* to bed.
Theresa, 6, Los Angeles, Calif.

When he comes upstairs to tuck us in, Dad says, "Fee Fi Fo Fum, I smell the blood of an Englishman." Every night.
Laurie, 9, Bethesda, Md.

Us and Them

37

They make me share a room with my nine-year-old
brother. I'd rather sleep in the laundry room.
Oh, not that I don't value him.
He's really excellent, for a fungus.
Ryan, 12, New Haven, Conn.

❧

They won't let me keep *my* stuff in *my* room the way
I want it. I don't like drawers or closets, okay?
I want my stuff in piles on the floor,
where I can *see* it and find it. But, *nooo*.
Doug, 16, White Plains, N.Y.

❧

Dad likes me to scratch his back. For, like, weeks at a
time. Months, if my nails would hold out. It's not so
bad, though. My sister has to rub his feet.
Sheila, 12, San Francisco, Calif.

Dad *loves* bathroom humor. Passing gas is his favorite topic. He'll do it and point to me or my brother, blame us. Meantime, small mammals and insects within five miles keel over and die.

Shawna, 15, Laguna Beach, Calif.

❧

If you look up "predictable" in the dictionary, you'll find my parents. Every day, they eat the same cornflakes, no deviations. When they argue, they each recite the same lines about the same stuff. They watch the same TV shows, never miss an episode of *ER*. They even go to the bathroom at exactly the same time every day.

Vanessa, 16, Evanston, Ill.

❧

My parents talk in pronouns. "Move this." "Get those for me." "Pick that up." Pick *what* up?

Mitch, 14, Reno, Nev.

Us and Them

There's no way to read my dad's handwriting.
If he leaves a note or a message—forget it.
Even *he* can't read it. If he gives me a grocery list,
I end up just guessing what's on it. He wrote
me letters at camp. I have no idea what they said.

Sheila, 12, Ft. Lauderdale, Fla.

✻

My mom puts orange juice on her cereal. Orange juice.

Dana, 10, Richmond, Va.

✻

There's no point talking to either of them in the
morning. They can't process information or deal with
anything. If you ask them a question, even, like,
to help you find a sweatshirt, they get confused, rattled.
Upset. Like they might blow a circuit.

Nate, 15, St. Louis, Mo.

They insist that I *eat* with them, just because it's
"mealtime." They make a fuss if I don't want to.
Like, what if I'm not hungry? Or not in the mood to
hear my baby brother smack his slimy lips and
watch him rub spaghetti in his hair?
Julie, 14, Miller, Ind.

Our kitchen's a graveyard for old food. *Nothing* gets
thrown out or "wasted." Leftovers get kept
until they've grown so much crud on them that
nobody can remember what they were.
Jerry, 16, Boulder, Colo.

The bad news is that Mom's not a great cook. The
good news is that Dad knows this. We eat out a lot.
Murray, 11, Shreveport, La.

Us and Them

41

Every time I sit down to eat, I hear,
"Don't use so much ketchup."
Drew, 11, Kansas City, Mo.

❦

My mom can put away an entire coconut cream pie.
For breakfast.
Midge, 15, Swarthmore, Pa.

❦

Mom keeps her kitchen spotless. Let's say you put
half a glass of milk on the counter.
Before you can get yourself a cookie, my mom'll have
washed the glass and put it away.
Dave, 9, Cincinnati, Ohio

Dad eats leftovers for breakfast. There you are,
just opening your eyes, and he's wolfing down cold
anchovy pizza or last week's moo goo gai pan.
Lizzie, 14, Washington, D.C.

❧

They always want me to try new stuff.
They'll say, "Try it. Just try." And they push it at me.
I don't even ask, anymore, what it is. I don't even want
to know. I just take a bite, swallow, and tell them
it's "delish." Then they leave me alone.
Paul, 10, Cherry Hill, N.J.

❧

At our house, if you don't like what's for dinner, you
can always have a bowl of cereal. I eat a lot of cereal.
Adam, 15, Cincinnati, Ohio

My mom's in law school. Dad cooks.
We eat lots of macaroni and cheese.

Mandy, 7, Evanston, Ill.

☙

My dad scratches his feet at the dinner table,
and my mom can't stand that. That's usually
what they talk about at dinner.

Alexis, 9, Fort Wayne, Ind.

My father and mother think we should have weekly "family meetings." Dad chairs them. He has an "agenda." We're supposed to communicate and "share" our problems and feelings, so we can all "hear" each other. Unfortunately, Dad refuses to "hear" what we say about the meetings.

Luke, 16, Minneapolis, Minn.

❧

My mom makes me keep lists. Write down my chores, homework, and whatever, and check things off as I do them. This is definitely a pain. But worse than that, just when I'm done, she adds things. "Clean out the hamster cage." Or, "Wash your hair." "Make tomorrow's list."

Gwen, 12, Charlottesville, Va.

❧

They believe that kids should have pets, but I'm allergic to everything. So they got me goldfish. Goldfish?

Hannah, 10, Los Angeles, Calif.

My mom's a cleanliness freak. Everything has to be
sterile. She washed the guinea pig cage with ammonia.
The cage got clean. The guinea pig died.
Eric, 10, St. Louis, Mo.

❧

There's a thing that goes on with my mom that I can't
define; I can only describe. For example, she'll shout,
"Larry—bring me the good scissors." I go to the
drawer and find, like, ten pairs of scissors in there.
How am I supposed to know which is the "good" one?
I pick one out—it looks pretty good to me—and I bring
it to her. She says, like she's talking to an idiot—
"Larry, I asked for the *good* scissors!"
Larry, 14, Buffalo, N.Y.

❧

My mom licks her fingers and
washes stuff off my face with her spit.
Meredith, 6, Escondido, Calif.

Every so often, my mom gets in a mood to clean.
It's scary. It's like barbarians are invading. Stuff's gone,
ripped away and thrown out before your eyes. You
hear her say, "You haven't played with this in years."
Before you can ask what "this" is, it's gone.
Scott, 11, Bethesda, Md.

❧

Mom likes blue. Our whole house is blue.
And everything in it.
Adam, 19, Kansas City, Mo.

❧

Mom loves to squeeze pimples.
When my skin breaks out, I have to lock my
bedroom door or hide in the closet.
Bob, 15, Niles, Ill.

My mom's nervous, so she keeps the doors locked.
We can be sitting on the front porch, and we need to
get a key to go in and answer the phone.
Holly, 13, Cherry Hill, N.J.

❧

When they're excited, my parents talk fast.
They rev up, wave their arms, interrupt each other.
You don't want to stand too close;
you can get whapped in the head.
Evan, 12, Portland, Oreg.

❧

They expect me to listen to and remember everything
they say. But they're *always* talking. So how can I listen
to everything? And if I ask them a question, half the
time, they won't answer me. They'll say, "We just told
you that. Why weren't you listening?"
Gena, 15, Rochester, N.Y.

My mom uses the wrong words. Like, she'll tell me
to bring my book bag instead of my swim bag,
then she'll be mad that I left my swim bag at home.
Or she'll tell me to go outside instead of upstairs.
My dad's no help; he says I should listen to
what she *means*, not what she says.
Elise, 11, Fort Wayne, Ind.

✧

My mom starts talking in the middle of a subject. She's
done the first half of the conversation in her head, but
she expects you to follow along and join in anyway.
Lacey, 10, Duluth, Minn.

✧

They can't throw things out. They still have
everything from when I was a baby. My blankets,
bath toys, mobiles, mittens. All the equipment
required for a complete childhood.
Jake, 14, Austin, Tex.

Mom's clothes are too geeky, so she wears mine.
Half of my stuff's in her room.
Cindy, 15, Philadelphia, Pa.

❧

They announce everything they do. They'll say, "I'm
going to the bathroom." Or, "I'm getting a drink." Or,
"I'm going downstairs." Like, what am I supposed to
do? Alert the media?
Will, 16, Radnor, Pa.

❧

They state the obvious. "It's getting dark." "It's cold
out." "It's time for lunch." When I'm 40, they'll
probably call me up to tell me, "It's raining."
Rick, 17, Skokie, Ill.

They have these things they *always* say. Like, every time
I go out, my dad says, "Don't do anything
I wouldn't do." He's also fond of, "If your friends
jumped off a bridge, would you jump, too?"
My mom says, "You spill, you die."
Clarke, 15, Indianapolis, Ind.

❧

They have stock phrases. Like, if I say something's not
fair, they'll say, "Life's not fair." Every time.
Together, like a chorus. Or if I lean back in my
chair at dinner, a pair of voices will say, "Lean over
your plate." You can count on it.
Dan, 12, New York, N.Y.

❧

Mom says, "Ask your father." Dad says, "Ask your
mother." Like I'm a Ping-Pong ball, back and forth.
Why can't one just talk to the other, save me the trips?
Diego, 10, Dallas, Tex.

Mom talks in clichés. Winning isn't everything.
A stitch in time saves nine. Honesty's the best policy.
Every cloud has a silver lining. I have one:
Every occasion has a cliché.
Lynda, 16, Grand Rapids, Mich.

❧

They don't listen to me. It's like a sitcom.
I told them I dented the car. They said, "Yes, dear.
That's nice, don't be late."
Mike, 19, Phoenix, Ariz.

❧

Nothing's ever settled. They discuss and debate and
redebate. There's always another "what if" or
"on the other hand" to consider. It can take my
parents three hours to decide what Chinese food to
order—and that's after they've spent two hours
deciding not to get Mexican.
Brad, 17, New York, N.Y.

They have the "Clapper." A bread-making machine.
A knitting machine. Phones in every shape and size.
The mop that's guaranteed to end all mops.
They watch that Home Shopping Network and,
    if there's a new gimmick, we own it.
But can I get a new pair of sneaks? Noooo.
Andrea, 18, St. Cloud, Minn.

❧

My mom collects little porcelain dolls and animals,
    little carved wooden figures. The house,
        every tabletop is full of munchkins.
If you have a glass of milk or snack, you have to hold it
    on your lap. There's no place to set it down.
Molly, 19, Miami, Fla.

Us and Them

53

One of them is always hanging over me while I do my homework. "No, that's not right. You forgot to carry the three." Then they'll argue about it. "Leave her alone, Dear. She'll remember the three if you give her some *time*."

Torie, 10, Wynnewood, Pa.

❧

My mom changes her mind all the time. She'll make a bed, decide she wants different sheets, and pull it apart. She makes U-turns on the highway. We might *think* we're going to the bank, but we'll stop and I'll get five inches of hair cut off on a whim, or we'll never make it to the supermarket because on the way we'll pass the library and she'll stop there instead. You never know who'll show up for dinner. She invites people, then forgets until they show up.

Rebecca, 14, New Hope, Pa.

My mom changes lanes suddenly, and she completely
ignores stop signs. You want to cover your eyes.
My dad curses the other drivers, yells at them out the
window. You want to cover your ears.
Alexandra, 14, Chevy Chase, Md.

They leave me silly notes in my bookbag or my lunch
box that have pretend rules on them.
Like, Rule #57: NEVER braid the bunny's ears.

Rosie, 8, San Jose, Calif.

❧

In the morning, they divide up the newspaper
and read articles out loud. They discuss them,
analyze them. Ask me what I think.

Doug, 12, Chicago, Ill.

❧

I have three sisters, so with my mom, there are five
females here. My dad calls us all "Woman." "Give me
a hug, Woman," or "Help me set the table, Woman."
He thinks it's cute. We, uh, don't.

Sophie, 11, Phoenix, Ariz.

"Please Don't Kiss Me
at the Bus Stop!"

56

It's not like they have eleven kids. They have three.
But they can't remember our names. They call me my
sister's and brother's names, even by each *other's*
names. I'm "David-I-mean-Carrie-I-mean-Suzy-
I-mean-Faye." Never just Faye.

Faye, 17, Santa Fe, N.Mex.

❧

My mom loses her keys. I mean, like, a few times
every day. She leaves them in the car, in the house,
in her other purse, in a jacket pocket. She can't ever
find them. Any time we go anywhere, we have
to wait until Mom can find her keys.

Elana, 13, Stamford, Conn.

❧

My dad spends an hour searching, tearing the house
apart. He growls, "Anybody seen my glasses?" They're
on a chain around his neck. Or sitting on his head. You
have to be diplomatic about how you point this out.

Grace, 16, Springfield, Mass.

They're always on the phone. We have two lines and,
if my parents are home, none of
my friends can call; both lines are always tied up.
Maybe they're talking to each other.
Toby, 13, New York, N.Y.

❧

There's real time and there's my mom's time, in which a
minute elongates and stretches like a rubberband. If she
says she'll be ready "in a minute," you know that, in
reality, she might be with you sometime this century.
Casey, 15, Amherst, Mass.

❧

They're always late picking me up places.
Wherever I go, I'm always the last one there.
Kim, 11, Escondido, Calif.

"One minute" can mean sometime next week.
Or, maybe, before Armageddon.
Unless they're giving *me* one minute.
Amy, 13, St. Petersburg, Fla.

%

My dad doesn't hear anything you say.
He's not deaf; he's on his own planet.
Arlene, 7, Green Bay, Wis.

%

I'm not allowed to interrupt. But I could grow a beard
before they stop talking. This can be bad if what
I want to say is important. Like, that a pot's boiling
over, or dinner's burning, or a man in a blue car
just drove off with my little sister.
Kevin, 10, Evanston, Ill.

Any place we go, they run into people they know.
Then they stop to chat. We never see the beginning
of a movie. I never get to soccer on time.
I can't wait to drive.
Sean, 13, Providence, R.I.

❧

My Mom's laugh is real shrill. You don't want
to stand near her. Or the windows.
Joe, 19, St. Paul, Minn.

❧

Dad snores so loud the walls shake. He denies it,
though; swears it's my mom. Or he'll say, "I wasn't
even sleeping. I was just resting my eyes."
Jason, 8, Claymont, Del.

"Please Don't Kiss Me
at the Bus Stop!"

60

Last summer, my mom backed over my bike—
no kidding—three times. No, actually, she backed
over three different bikes, one time each.

Steve, 9, Buffalo Grove, Ill.

❧

Mom starts every sentence with, "Yeah, because..."
as if she's in a conversation with herself. "Yeah,
because it might rain..." "Yeah, because we're out of
milk..." "Yeah, because whatever..."

Walt, 19, Erie, Pa.

❧

If you don't answer my mother the *instant* she
finishes talking, she repeats herself. And she keeps on
repeating herself until you answer.

Tony, 17, Albuquerque, N.Mex.

They change the subject in the middle. They both do.
Mom'll be talking about fixing up the yard and Dad
will ask what everyone wants for dessert.
Then Mom'll say he needs to get a haircut and he'll
comment about why the White Sox lost.
Without a pause, Mom'll say she ran into our old
neighbor at the cleaners. There's no way to follow a
conversation. Well, there *is* no conversation.

Barb, 18, Chicago, Ill.

✣

Dad runs and he gets all sweaty. Then he chases me
and my mom to get a hug. Iieeuwuw!

Stephanie, 6, Indianapolis, Ind.

✣

Dad loves to talk about his childhood.

Brad, 19, Cleveland, Ohio

My dad talks to me in this real high falsetto.
"Hi, Janie! How was school today, Janie?"
He sounds like a manic parrot.
Jane, 15, St. Paul, Minn.

They cry at books, at movies. TV commercials.
Dad, even more than Mom. We're talking boxes
of tissues. If you ask Dad if he's all right, he gets
macho, snaps at you, "Leave it alone!"
Mark, 12, Cleveland, Ohio

They don't let me wear what I want. They buy me
dorky stuff. *Dresses*. With *lace*.
Kelly, 7, Stamford, Conn.

My mom carries half-used old kleenexes up her sleeves.
When she hugs me, damp,
mushy kleenexes fall out, everywhere.
Evelyn, 12, Nashville, Tenn.

❧

Whatever show I'm watching, they say I'm brain-dead
from watching it. If they see me *near* a television,
they say, "Why don't you do your homework,
set the table, walk the dog, practice your flute?"
I gave up flute three years ago.
Brenda, 13, Toledo, Ohio

❧

They love junk food. Donuts, pizza, chips, candy,
cookies. For them, exercise is to walk to the kitchen.
John, 15, Marlton, N.J.

They smoke. Our whole house stinks.
Even my *clean* clothes smell like an old ashtray.
Lindsey, 14, Louisville, Ky.

❧

They're teaching me to drive. So far,
nobody's committed a violent crime, but I *might*
be an orphan before I get my license.
Katie, 16, Downers Grove, Ill.

❧

Mom gets lost when she drives. She calls my dad on the
car phone. They have long panicky discussions.
"Where am I? How do I get out of here?"
Generally, you need to leave an extra half hour when
she's taking you somewhere.
Bryan, 13, Newark, Del.

They have this thing about mileage.
They check the odometer and the gas gauge and
then do the arithmetic to find out how many miles they
get per gallon. And then they get thrilled, I mean
happy, if it's over twenty-two.
Raymond, 14, Tulsa, Okla.

House Rules

From breakfast to bedtime, in public or private, sickness or health, children are dominated by adults. They're told to mind their manners, wait their turns, be still, sit down, stand up, stand up straighter, say please, say thank you, be quiet, speak up. And if they don't obey, they face consequences.

No matter how hard parents try to be consistent, fair, and reasonable, the logic behind their rules tends to elude their children. Limits often seem arbitrary or absurd, discipline random or ridiculous.

For some kids, rules are unpredictable, changing with a blink of an eye, a sibling's whine, or a parent's whim. Nothing is carved in stone. And nothing, therefore, is beyond negotiation.

For others, their parents' rules are rigidly inflexible. "Bedtime's nine o'clock," says Dean, ten. "No matter what. I can have three pages left to my book. Or ten minutes left to a video. Lights out."

Whether their parents are strict or lenient, many kids live in hopes that, if they remain consistent, fair, and reasonable, their parents will eventually wise up, ease up, and lighten up. Others are more resigned, accepting the fact that some things in life—like their parents' rules—are merely to be accepted, not understood.

ॐ

My mom believes in bananas. Every day, everybody must eat half a banana. No matter what.
Ellie, 9, Detroit, Mich.

You've got to squeeze the toothpaste from
the bottom of the tube. If you squeeze from the top
or the middle, my father goes nuts.

Nate, 11, Denver, Colo.

My sister and I have curfews.
I asked my mom why. She said because,
when she was growing up, she had them.
She thinks that makes sense.

Dena, 15, Naples, Fla.

We can't answer the phone until the third ring.

Felicia, 9, New Orleans, La.

They'll yell at me and actually send me to my room
right in front of my friends.

Kevin, 8, Portland, Oreg.

⳾

I have to be home by dark. If it's one second after,
my father'll stand on the front step and call, "SUSAN!"
The whole neighborhood can hear.

Susan, 9, Pennington, N.J.

⳾

All closet doors *must* be closed. All drawers and
cabinets must be closed. Nothing can be on the top
of a desk or a counter. If I put a plate out, my mom'll
put it away before I can make myself a sandwich.
The house has to look like nobody *lives* here.

Tom, 14, Bryn Mawr, Pa.

I'm not allowed to go to the mall. Everybody goes
to the mall, all my friends. But nooo. Not me.
Lindsey, 14, Bridgewater, N.J.

"Make your bed, brush your teeth, get in the car."
Every morning, I hear that. Every morning.
Bert, 11, Highland Park, Ill.

"Seat belts." They say that every time I get in the car.
I'm twelve years old. I've been hearing that for twelve
years, maybe thirty times a week. So, what's that,
almost twenty thousand times? You'd think that,
by now, they'd trust me to remember? Especially since,
by the time they say it, I've already got it buckled.
Gary, 12, Evanston, Ill.

Whenever I go anywhere,
even the front yard, my mom yells,
"BE CAREFUL!"
Samantha, 7, Wayne, Pa.

We're not allowed to put our feet on the coffee table,
or to eat or drink on the couch. Only Dad can.
He's "The Man of the House." And he gets the
cozy corner of the couch, too.
Meredith, 7, Glenview, Ill.

No one's allowed to sit on Dad's part of the sofa.
If you do and he comes in, you better
scootch over. Fast.
Bryan, 13, Raleigh, N.C.

They wake me up at 7:30 A.M. every day. Oh, wait.
That's not true. On *Saturdays*, they let me sleep in.
They don't wake me up till eight.

Marissa, 14, Seattle, Wash.

In our family, you have to wear a hat in winter.
My mom tells you that 77 percent of your body heat
gets lost through your head. Or something like that.
Even if you're sweating, have to wear a hat. She'll chase
you down the street if you take it off.

Derek, 9, Utica, N.Y.

No shoes in the house. No matter what.
If you have to throw up or go to the bathroom,
you still have to take your shoes off first.

Steve, 12, Stamford, Conn.

Whose fingerprints are on the mirror? Who drew
pictures on the car windows? Who ate my chicken leg?
Who spilled orange juice on the counter?
Like they have to blame somebody for every little thing.
Ashley, 10, Deerfield, Ill.

❧

You have to put paper on the toilet seat unless
you're home. At a restaurant, the airport,
wherever we are, as I'm going to the Ladies' Room,
I hear, "PUT PAPER ON THE SEAT!"
Jessica, 9, Portsmouth, Va.

❧

"Wash your hands?" They say that every time
I come out of the bathroom.
Ed, 12, Bethesda, Md.

If we use public bathrooms, my mom warns us not to touch anything. She tells us to use our feet to flush. Wash with soap, and then cover the door handle with a paper towel when you open the door to leave.

Marsha, 11, New York, N.Y.

ॐ

They always back each other up, even when one is wrong and the other knows it. They're like Siamese twins, or clones. It's like they think they have to agree, show a united front, or we'll stage a coup.

Andrea, 17, Montgomery, Ala.

ॐ

No matter how wrong they are, they never apologize. Never.

Vanessa, 12, Miller, Ind.

They want me to finish everything. "Clean your plate,
James." Thank God we have a dog.
James, 12, Madison, Wis.

❧

I've got to clean my plate. Eat everything,
even if it's green. And I have to swallow it.
Mary, 6, Atlanta, Ga.

❧

At our house, if you make your bed, clear your plate,
put your stuff away, and wipe up the sink when you
brush your teeth, you've pretty much got it made.
Gabrielle, 8, Albany, N.Y.

❧

My mom has numbers for everything you do.
Chew your food a hundred times. Brush your hair a
hundred times. Brush your teeth to a hundred and fifty.
Count to ten when you get mad.
Denise, 12, Rochester, N.Y.

Rules change, based on what Mom reads in the paper on any given day. "You're not driving alone after dark," she'll say. "Look what happened—a girl got murdered on the highway." When a woman got raped while jogging, my mom declared that I must never wear a Walkman on the street. "The Walkman's why she got raped," Mom said. "She couldn't hear him come up behind her." If an airplane crashes, she tells me not to fly. And I'm not allowed to go to California, ever. She's heard about the earthquakes.

Donna, 17, Fort Wayne, Ind.

❧

My mom gets mad when I get hurt. She scolds me. "Be more careful! Stop hurting yourself." When I get sick, she says, "Wash your hands once in a while, you won't get germs in your mouth." Like I got sick on purpose.

Scott, 9, Salinas, Calif.

If I trip or stumble, my mom says, "Always know
where your body parts are." Or sometimes she says,
"No one can keep track of your feet but you, Dear."
Lois, 9, Houston, Tex.

If I go in the kitchen after school—
if I even *look* at the kitchen—my mom yells,
"NO SWEETS BEFORE DINNER!"
Katie, 8, Raleigh, N.C.

Every day when I come home, before
I even get my jacket off, I hear,
"NO TV UNTIL YOUR HOMEWORK'S DONE!"
Brad, 11, Pittsburgh, Pa.

"Please Don't Kiss Me
at the Bus Stop!"

78

I have to do my homework before I can go outside.
But, by the time I do my homework,
it's too late to go outside.

Wesley, 10, Gladwyne, Pa.

❧

"Homework, piano, walk the dog." That's my welcome
home every day. Not, "Hi, Laurie. Did you have a good
day? Would you like a snack? How do you feel?" No.
I get, "Hey, Laurie—homework, piano, walk the dog."

Laurie, 9, Laurel, Miss.

❧

When they're mad, they count. "One.... Two...." If
they get to three, they say that there are going to be
consequences. I have no idea what "consequences" are,
but they sound bad, so I never let them get to three.

Jeremy, 7, Salina, Kans.

If I'm doing my homework and I ask them
how to spell a word, they tell me, "Look it up in the
dictionary." I have to stop what I'm doing,
go get a dictionary, spend so much time looking up a
word that I forget my whole train of thought.
They will not tell me, even though they know.
Like it would hurt them. Like I'd get some
permanent character flaw if they told me if
dependent ends in "ent" or "ant."

Lorrie, 16, Naples, Fla.

&

"Stand up straight. Get off the phone!
Get out of the bathroom. Watch your mouth.
Change your tone of voice, young lady." What else?
Oh, "Don't crack your gum. File your nails."
Basically, there's a rule against everything I do.

Marissa, 15, Norwich, Conn.

If you talk back, they'll say, "That's it! You're not going to camp next summer." Or, if you didn't clean your room, they'll say you can't watch television till November. Nothing they say has anything to do with real life.

Alex, 11, Bridgeport, Conn.

❧

They make threats. "If you spill on that dress, I'm never buying you another good outfit." "If you don't behave, we're never going out to dinner again." "Go to sleep or this will be your last sleepover ever." "Young lady, you've just watched your last television show." Like I'm scared. They can't possibly *mean* any of this stuff.

Dolly, 10, Austin, Tex.

❧

They bribe me. "Don't expect a puppy for your birthday if you don't clean your room." Or, "If you want a raise in your allowance, you better get good grades."

Jimmy, 9, Santa Cruz, Calif.

It's always, "No." No matter what I'm asking.
I don't think they ever even listen to the question.
Before I get it out, one of them says, "No."
It's like: "Mom? Dad?"
"NO!"
Nicole, 15, Fort Wayne, Ind.

❧

They're big on "Sir" and "Ma'am." You can get
away with a lot if you just say, "Please, sir."
Or, "Thank you, Ma'am."
Scott, 9, New Orleans, La.

❧

They never let me stay up late because if I do, my little
sister will want to, too. But if she gets to do
something—like have a sleepover—and I want to do
it also, they say, "Don't expect everything to be equal."
Lucy, 11, Denver, Colo.

My mother won't let me go swimming in our neighbors' pools, in case some little kids might have peed in them. I'm not supposed to drink from public water fountains or use pay phones unless it's a dire emergency, and then don't touch anything to my skin. She tells me to carry a spray can of disinfectant in my pocketbook, not to use a public toilet unless I spray the seat first.
Heather, 17, St. Louis, Mo.

Every night before dinner, my dad says grace. At the end, he says, "Amen. Marla, lean over your plate."
Marla, 6, Springfield, Mo.

At our house, you have to eat breakfast. They say, "Breakfast is not optional."
Dwayne, 8, Dallas, Tex.

House Rules

I'm not allowed to have marshmallow cereal. Ever.
Meghan, 7, Glenview, Ill.

I'm not allowed to lick my dessert dish.
Even if there's icing on it. Even fudge.
Elissa, 9, Salinas, Calif.

My dad won't let me mush my ice cream into soup.
He says it's too messy. I think this is unfair on his part,
but he will not listen to my side.
Ruthanne, 8, Norfolk, Va.

When we have ice cream sundaes, I'm allowed
only one kind of syrup. Maybe whipped cream,
but no gummy bears. Ever.
Stacey, 9, Tallahassee, Fla.

To go to grandma's, you have to wear a suit. Even in
the summer. Even for a barbecue.
Louis, 9, Somerville, N.J.

❧

We aren't supposed to eat the last bite of
our food or take the last portion of anything,
or we'll be old maids. We're not supposed to read
at the dinner table or we'll get cross-eyed
husbands. If I say these are just stupid superstitions,
Mom says, "Maybe. But what's the sense of testing?"
Nina, 16, Cicero, Ill.

❧

At our house, candy's an illegal substance. Mom and
Dad open their mouths and show us all the fillings they
got, how they ruined their teeth with candy.
Which means, when they were kids, *they* got to eat
whatever they wanted. It's *so* unfair.
Tonika, 11, Syracuse, N.Y.

My mother never lets me have soda for lunch, and I'm in fifth grade! They always want me to do what's "good" for me, and this makes me really mad.

Samantha, 10, Bryn Mawr, Pa.

❧

No blue nail polish. Or yellow. Or green. Not even if I pay for it with my own allowance money.

Serena, 10, Toledo, Ohio

❧

My mom gives orders like an army officer. Half the time, she makes no sense. Like she'll say, "No more bike riding today," and if I ask her why, she'll say, "Because I said so." Or, "Because I'm your mother." She also says, "What Mother says goes." If anything ever goes wrong—like a kid on our street broke his arm—she says, "See what happens when you don't listen to your mother?"

Sam, 10, Richmond, Va.

Whenever we're leaving somebody's house or a party, they say, "What do you say?" or "Say thank you," as if I'm a complete social dolt or doofus. Like I'd never have thought of saying "Thank you" on my own?

Kim, 11, Madison, Wis.

❧

My mother has all these rules about how to go through life. "Look at the bright side." "Do what you can do." "You'll catch flies with honey, not vinegar." If something goes wrong, she says, "Let that be a lesson." If she catches you feeling smug, she says, "Pride goeth before a fall."

Brooke, 19, Boston, Mass.

❧

You have to use correct grammar. If I say "I" instead of "me" or "me" instead of "I," they go nuts. They don't get it that kids, like, don't talk that way.

Gwen, 13, New York, N.Y.

Anything I want to do, my mom says, "Fine. That's
Plan A. But always have a Plan B, in case that doesn't
work. What's your Plan B?" This can apply to anything. Going to college at Harvard or spending a day at
the the beach. Probably, when I introduce her to a guy
I want to marry, she'll ask, "What's your Plan B?"
Gigi, 18, Elmira, N.Y.

❧

They say, "Be yourself," but they won't let me
pierce my nose. They tell me, "Have fun,"
but come home by twelve. They say, "Relax,"
but make me turn down my music so low I can't even
hear it. There's always a "but."
Lois, 17, Little Rock, Ark.

❧

Dad yells, "QUIET!" Mom screams,
"INSIDE VOICES, PLEASE!"
Sam, 9, Pittsburgh, Pa.

They keep track of the times they yell at us, like a
scoreboard. Each time you get in trouble, they take a
dime off your allowance. This can get expensive. Some
weeks, I end up owing *them* money.

Steven, 11, Denver, Colo.

❧

Every so often, Mom makes you do stuff with her.
You have to go keep her company. It might be a walk,
or a bike ride. Or it could be a shopping spree.
But it's required, you can't say no. It's usually worth it,
though. I mean, if you go along, she'll get you
an ice cream or something.

Jessica, 14, Grand Rapids, Mich.

❧

Whenever I take a step, they say,
"Pick your feet up. Don't drag your feet!"
Diane, 14, Bethesda, Md.

Ever since I learned to walk, Mom says,
"Take your time, go slowly, watch what you're doing,
and think." She says it like it's one word.
Sheldon, 10, Fort Wayne, Ind.

❧

"Do as I say, not as I do." That's my dad's standard
rule. So he gets to sleep in on weekends, eat pizza for
breakfast, and put off chores. Whatever he wants.
Tim, 16, Pittsburgh, Pa.

❧

My mother is always telling us never to
talk to other people about politics, religion, money,
or members of your family.
Susan, 12, Brooklyn, N.Y.

❧

"Never tell anybody something you wouldn't want to
read about in the newspaper." That's what my mom says.
Alexandra, 14, Chevy Chase, Md.

My mom's always saying, "Cut it out." Cut *what* out?
Or "Stop it." Stop what? I don't have a clue what she's
talking about. "Sit still," she'll say. I *was* sitting still.

Evan, 11, Los Angeles, Calif.

❧

I'm always the one who has to be sociable. Call
Grandma. Call Aunt Bess. It would cheer up Uncle Phil
to hear from you, why don't you write him a letter?
Aunt Myrna's on the phone, she wants to say hello.
I didn't even know I *had* an Aunt Myrna.

Pamela, 11, Lexington, Ky.

❧

I get all the disgusting chores. Clean the litterbox,
wash the bathtub. Put the dirty clothes in the bin.
All my sister has to do is, like, put her crayons away.

Sophie, 10, Rochester, N.Y.

Each kid in our house has a list of chores, so we'll learn to Be Responsible and Do Our Share. My brother pays me to do his. So far, I've made over seventeen dollars.

Marty, 9, Cincinnati, Ohio

I'm like a prisoner. They don't want me to tie up their phone, but they won't let me get my own. I get allotted phone time. One call, ten minutes, then back to your cell.

Andrea, 12, Doylestown, Pa.

Rules are rules, unless my mom's in the mood to break them. Like, bedtime is nine o'clock. But if, suddenly, Mom's in the mood for fresh donuts in the middle of the night, bedtime gets blown away.

Bart, 10, St. Louis, Mo.

I'm not supposed to say some things in front of people.
Like bathroom things. Or somebody's perfume smelling
bad. How much money things cost. Things like that.

Selena, 7, St. Cloud, Minn.

❧

If you're sad, Mom says, "Don't dwell on your
troubles. It only makes things worse." She acts like
you can make your problems go away just
by not thinking about them.

Blake, 13, Jackson, Miss.

❧

Mom always says not to be beholden to anybody.
What this means is, "When you wake up each morning,
you should feel like there isn't anybody in the
world you can't tell to go to hell."

Raymond, 14, Tulsa, Okla.

Everything has to be put away. Everything. Table tops must be clear. If a toy's out, you might not see it again, for months. If your shoes or, maybe, your hairbrush are out, you'll find them stuffed under your pillow.

Laura, 9, Indianapolis, Ind.

❧

They say they want me to be open and honest and talk to them, but they really don't want to know what's going on if it's bad. They can't stand it if I have a problem, really can't stand to hear anything negative. Instead of helping me find actual solutions, they rephrase things, describe my situation in a way that makes it sound good, even when it sucks.
A "problem" becomes a "challenge." A "bully" turns into "a troubled kid." A fascist teacher is "an opportunity to get along with all types of people."

Lyle, 17, Chicago, Ill.

No matter what you do, you get grounded.
Come in late, forget to straighten your room, leave the
gas tank empty. Whatever. They say, "You do the
crime, you do the time." You're grounded.
Paul, 16, Winston-Salem, N.C.

❧

My mom hates snow. She won't let me go
out on snowy days. Even if school's open,
she won't let me go to school.
Shane, 11, Villanova, Pa.

❧

Dad can't answer anything in less than a speech. Don't
expect him to say, "yes" or "no." He can't. He's
unable. If you ask my dad for something, the least you
can hope for is a few paragraphs that translate into
"Maybe." Which translates into "Ask your mom."
Ben, 15, Chicago, Ill.

Dad gives the same lecture every time he gets mad. About kids today, values in our country, the whole nine yards. He can't just be mad that you called your sister a name. He has to put it in terms of the universe. He can't stop in the middle, either. There's no short version. All you can do, once he gets started, is roll your eyes, wait it out, and apologize.

Gabe, 15, Kansas City, Mo.

※

I get in trouble because my parents don't get it. Kids don't deal with stuff like grown-ups do. You gotta be a kid to know. Sometimes you've got to break the rules, otherwise you're just a dweeb. If somebody's pushing you all the time, you can't just "talk it out." Sometimes you gotta shove him back. Hard.

Alex, 9, Costa Mesa, Calif.

CHAPTER 4

Little "Pitchers"

It's said that children don't miss much. Like sponges, they absorb everything around them. In the intimacy of family life, they inevitably pick up information that their parents would prefer them to overlook; after all, even parents need *some* borders and privacy.

To hear children tell it, however, it is not they but their parents who burst through barriers, invade personal space, trample territory, and ignore the dignified privacy of family members. Well-intentioned but often insensitive, Mom and Dad blunder through bathroom doors, interrupt phone conversations, make public references to private matters. In bathrooms and bedrooms, eating meals or reading mail, parents let cats out of bags, skeletons out of closets, dirty laundry into the air.

"My mom thinks keeping secrets is like lying," says Marsha, sixteen. "She doesn't get the difference between 'secret' and 'private,' and she tells her friends everything. One of them saw me at the mall and told me how glad she was I finally broke up with my boyfriend. I don't even know her name, but she's all over me, saying, 'Don't worry. There's plenty more fish in the sea.'"

For better or worse, family life provides ample room for infringements of privacy by parents and children alike. According to some kids, however, the main problem isn't little pitchers that have big ears; more often, it's parents that have big mouths.

⚬

They knock and walk right in.
They don't wait for the *come in* part.
Stephanie, 11, Atlanta, Ga.

My room is supposed to be *my* room, right?
But my mom thinks she can just walk
right in and clean it out any time she wants.
She touches my stuff. Rearranges it.
Craig, 13, Fargo, N.D.

❧

They let my little brother mess with my stuff.
I come home from school and my room's a disaster.
He's been into everything. I have to hide stuff
on the top shelf of the closet, even in my own room.
If I complain, Mom says, "He's only three
years old. What harm can he do?"
Marc, 11, Cleveland, Ohio

❧

They come in my room right when I'm playing
with my dollhouse. They talk to me right in the middle.
They ask me how my dolls are, and if any of
them are being bad or sick.
Libby, 6, Des Moines, Iowa

Little "Pitchers"

I'm in the bathroom with the door closed.
My mom yells, "Ronald, what are you doing in
there for so long?" Like, what does she *think*
I'm doing in there for so long?

Ronald, 14, St. Paul, Minn.

I hate to take a shower after my dad.
There are all these hairs stuck in the soap.

Jennifer, 10, Boca Raton, Fla.

When I'm in the bathroom, my mother stands outside
the door and says, "You know, going to the bathroom
isn't supposed to be a full-time job." And she acts like
it's a crime if there's a loose hair in the sink.

Ashton, 14, Boston, Mass.

Whenever I go in bathroom, someone starts banging
on the door. I can't ever just go in peace.
Wendy, 15, Buffalo, N.Y.

Mom sniffs me to make sure I'm wearing deodorant.
Rosie, 11, Providence, R.I.

Mom searches my skin for pimples. When she
talks to me, she's scanning my forehead, nose,
anyplace that can break out.
Wendy, 14, Jackson, Miss.

Mom checks my hair, like she's looking for lice.
In front of people. Just anyplace, for no reason.
Allyson, 8, Cherry Hill, N.J.

Every night, my mother asks, "Did you poop today?" If I didn't, she asks me again in the morning. She doesn't let up on this until I tell her, yes, it's okay, I pooped. And then she starts all over again the next night.
Larry, 10, Southfield, Mich.

❧

Every morning, Mom asks, "Did you brush your teeth?" Then she sticks a finger in my mouth and scrapes a tooth to see if there's any yellow stuff.
Mitch, 7, Detroit, Mich.

❧

My mom still cuts my toenails.
She will *not* let me do it myself.
Eric, 10, Pittsburgh, Pa.

If I went into my mom's purse, she'd have a fit.
But she goes right into my book bag,
empties it out, asks me about every single note
or nickel or candy wrapper.
Denise, 11, Wilmington, Del.

Sometimes my dad doesn't flush.
He denies it, says it wasn't him.
Bonnie, 10, Des Plaines, Ill.

Dad stinks up the bathroom. Seriously.
Sometimes we have to evacuate the first floor.
Dean, 14, Springfield, Mo.

Dad doesn't shave on the weekends, and when he kisses me, he scrapes my face. He feels like splinters.

Sarah, 7, Framingham, Mass.

❧

Mom tells us to conserve water by sharing baths and taking showers together. With my sister. And she wants us to flush only for number two.

Elana, 9, San Francisco, Calif.

❧

Veins, wrinkles, grey hair. Thigh bulge. Arm flab. Bags under her eyes. Mom stands at her mirror, shakes her head, and lists this stuff. "Look at my saggy boobs. My bottom's completely flat." Dad looks at her and licks his lips. Please.

Stacey, 16, Memphis, Tenn.

When Mom gets "the curse," watch out.
Don't go near her, if you can help it.
Sondra, 8, Kansas City, Mo.

Every so often, Mom says, "I have my friend."
Then she stays in bed all day.
Keith, 9, Charlotte, N.C.

First my mom complained about cramps,
now it's hot flashes. It's me who's got the cramps.
Laurie, 17, Wichita, Kans.

My mom gets her cramps, retains water.
She tells me I'm lucky to be a boy.
Peter, 11, Cheyenne, Wyo.

Little "Pitchers"

105

Mom told me about periods and all, but she never said
you *keep* getting your period every *month*.
Renee, 12, Philadelphia, Pa.

❦

I got my period when I was ten.
The whole world knew. My mom was on the
phone telling my aunt, my grandma,
her best friend, Kate. She even told my *father*.
Candace, 13, Munster, Ind.

❦

Mom keeps track of my periods.
She charts them on a calendar. In the *kitchen*.
Holly, 13, Wichita, Kans.

There are code words at our house. Real language
embarrasses them. Girls have a "Hmhmhm" or "Tuss."
Boys have "wangs," "weenies," or "Johnsons."
Periods are "George."
Phyllis, 18, Chevy Chase, Md.

❧

You can't embarrass my dad. Not even by
walking in on him when he's peeing. He just
blinks at you, keeps on peeing.
Stu, 8, Bridgeport, Conn.

❧

Dad sleeps naked. Even in the winter.
Rory, 6, Atlanta, Ga.

Dad never cuts his toenails.
I swear, they're three inches long.
Eric, 9, Toledo, Ohio

My mom trims my dad's nose hairs, also the hair
growing out of his ears. Right in front of us.
Tory, 9, Tallahassee, Fla.

Mom's always at her magnifying mirror,
tweezing and squeezing.
Beth, 15, Atlanta, Ga.

Dad trims the hairs under his arms. Hello?
Fran, 13, Tampa, Fla.

Don't go near the bathroom when my dad's
shaving unless you want shaving cream all over your
face, in your hair and ears, and on your shirt.
He's a wild man. He thinks this is fun.
Savannah, 12, Los Angeles, Calif.

You don't want to go into my dad's bathroom alone.
It's scary. The sink's coated with the skuzz from when
he shaves. Little pieces of his whiskers in cream.
I swear, there's new life forms growing in that stuff.
Mona, 17, Scarsdale, N.Y.

Dad acts like a kid. He's like, "Oh, wow! Ice cream!"
Or he turns up the radio, "I *love* this song!"
He'd get his ear pierced if Mom would let him.
Alex, 9, Wilmette, Ill.

My dad had hair transplants.
Now he thinks he's cool, dresses flashy.
Neal, 15, St. Louis, Mo.

❧

Dad worries about losing his hair.
He stands at the mirror, rearranging it. He examines
his comb, counts the casualties.
Dave, 15, Austin, Tex.

My dad has nightgowns in his closet.
Just like my mom's.
Jenna, 12, Fort Wayne, Ind.

My mom lies all the time. But if I contradict what
she says or correct her, she gets mad at me and says
I embarrassed her and ruined her story.
Carly, 10, Cherry Hill, N.J.

You can tell when Mom's lying because whenever she
lies, she swears on Great Grandma Sylvia's grave.
Barbara, 13, Portland, Maine

I know when my mom doesn't like
somebody, because when they call she makes
me tell them she's in the shower.
Amy, 8, Phoenix, Ariz.

Little "Pitchers"

111

My mom drove around the block to avoid letting
a black cat cross our path. She broke the mirror in her
blush-on and was upset for days. But then she
found a heads-up penny. That helped.
Celia, 14, Minneapolis, Minn.

&

Mom and Dad whisper to each other. "Pspspsps."
What is it I'm not supposed to hear? I'm the only
other one in room. They giggle and whisper, whisper
and giggle. Is it about me? Is it something
I don't *want* to know? It's rude.
Elliot, 15, Southfield, Mich.

&

They have a secret whistle for each other.
Instead of calling each other, they tweet.
Like a pair of sick lovebirds.
Al, 14, Cincinnati, Ohio

Sometimes, in the middle of the night, my dad shouts
the weirdest things. I swear, he goes, "Tally ho!"
Or something like that. It wakes me up, but if I ask him
about it the next morning, he says he doesn't
know what I'm talking about.
Janice, 7, Charlottesville, Va.

❧

We found balloons in daddy's nightstand but he
got mad and wouldn't blow them up. He told us
never to touch his nightstand anymore.
Evie, 6, Vineland, N.J.

❧

They French kiss. Yuck.
Dana, 6, Orlando, Fla.

Mom and Dad call each other Dooby and Fuzz. I don't
know what the Dooby's about, but I get the Fuzz.
Jason, 14, Louisville, Ky.

They leave condom wrappers in the trashcans. In plain
sight, where anybody who looks in the trash can see
them. I don't get it. I mean, don't they think about
that? Why don't they, like, throw them *out* someplace?
Gordon, 15, Providence, R.I.

Dad gave me a condom. "Carry this in
your wallet," he said, "so when the time comes,
you'll be prepared." I stood there like a total dork.
I couldn't think of anything to say, so I just sort
of took it and put it in my wallet.
Steve, 14, San Diego, Calif.

They talk about whether or not to have another kid.
They ask my brother and me what we think,
because they say time is running out and Mom will
only be fertile a few more years. Um. Do I have to think
about this? I mean, is this my job?

Ian, 15, Escondido, Calif.

❧

My mom told me I should start to wear a bra.
I mean, she wants to take me shopping. For bras.
I told her, no way. I mean, no way. I told her
to please not talk about it anymore.

Debra, 11, Chevy Chase, Md.

❧

Mom had me take this Pencil Test. Then she said I can
wear bras if I want to, but that they ride up and feel
like a harness and, if I have any sense at all, I'll throw
them out or not buy any to begin with.

Rena, 12, Tulsa, Okla.

Mom stands at the mirror, posing in her underwear.
She says, "Not bad for an old broad, huh?"
Lisa, 14, Decatur, Ill.

❧

I'm with my boyfriend, in the den. Actually, we're
kissing. My mom walks in, talking to me. She turns on
the lights and keeps talking even when she sees his
hand in my blouse. She stands in the doorway,
talking like nothing unusual's going on.
Melanie, 18, Valley Forge, Pa.

❧

They don't close their door. Once I walked in on them.
Mom screamed. Dad gasped and fell off the bed
onto the floor. He landed on his head. I got in my car
and drove around for a few hours.
We all pretended it never happened.
Rob, 17, Evanston, Ill.

Mom's always cold, and she uses me to warm her
hands. She puts them under my sweater, up my back.
Ned, 16, Portland, Oreg.

❦

Constipation? Diarrhea? Hemorrhoids? Theirs. Mine.
Yours. Anyone's. These are my parents' fave topics.
Sally, 14, Tampa, Fla.

❦

When Dad worries, he bites his nails. When Mom
worries, she grinds her teeth. Nobody talks about this.
If you say, "What's wrong?" they just bite and
grind and say, "Nothing. Why?"
Dawn, 20, New Orleans, La.

Dad pours cheap Scotch into a Chivas bottle. When
I asked why, he said, "Because the Chivas bottle's so
much prettier than the others." Like, right, Dad.

Len, 17, Grand Rapids, Mich.

&

All they talk about is how much things cost. Bargains.
The best deal on trips to Florida, how much the
neighbor got for trading in his old car, the cheapest
dry cleaner. The value of getting mustard in
giant jars as opposed to little ones.

Valerie, 14, Washington, D.C.

&

Never try to exchange a gift from my mom.
She wraps presents she bought at the Dollar Store in
Nordstrom's or Bloomingdale's boxes.

Edie, 15, Wayne, Pa.

Dad always has to impress everyone. He has to think he's a big shot. Like, before a concert or a play, he struts up the aisle about a hundred times, checking the time on his ten-pound Rolex, making sure everyone saw him in his thousand-dollar suit.

Frank, 17, Highland Park, Ill.

❧

Dad says that everyone's a little bit dishonest. People who aren't are fools. The IRS expects you to cheat a little bit. Clients know you've added an hour or two to their fees. And the boss knows you're going to take home paper and a bunch of pens.

It's normal.

Claude, 14, Chestnut Hill, Mass.

❧

My dad wears a girdle.
He says it's for his back, but I don't think so.

Cheryl, 14, Lexington, Ky.

Mom wants me to have "the right" friends.
Life is tough, she says, so you need to know the right
people; that's how things work. Don't hang around
with a "nobody." But nobody's probably the only
one who'd be good enough for her.

Francine, 17, New Canaan, Conn.

❧

My mom weighs herself about eight times a day.
At least, after every meal. Then she goes,
"Tsk," or "damn," and swears the scale's
off by six or eight pounds.

Alexandra, 11, Fort Wayne, Ind.

❧

When Dad works out, he asks us to measure
his muscles afterwards. While he's "pumped."
This is seriously disgusting.

Laurie, 15, Boulder, Colo.

Dad has sinus problems, and he honks all the time.
When he blows his nose, ships at sea must think
it's a fog horn. When he sneezes,
you want to take cover. The dog hides.

Hal, 14, Salinas, Calif.

Dad's always in a rush. If he has to wait,
he, like, goes nuts, paces around, and jingles his
keys, twitches, cracks his knuckles, bounces
his knees. He makes you crazy.
Lynne, 17, Tulsa, Okla.

My dad snuggles the guinea pig, nose to nose.
He sings to her when he thinks no one's around.
Anne, 8, Raleigh, N.C.

They have a shelf of really dirty books in the back
of their closet. Really dirty. My brother found them
back there, because the back of his closet's
where he keeps *his* dirty books.
Eddie, 11, Pittsburgh, Pa.

My mom calls my dad's mother Haggalinah.
His sister's Baggalinah.
Jodie, 10, Fayetteville, N.C.

❧

Aunt Jo touches my dad all the time, and she says she'll
do anything for him. She says if he ever dumps my
mom, she's ready. Mom says Jo can have Dad any time.
Mandy, 14, Orlando, Fla.

❧

They don't tell us kids anything. You have to listen to
their phone conversations if you want to find out
what's going on. Dentist appointments. What's for dinner. Most of it's boring, but if you wait a while, you'll
hear what you want. Like whether they're still mad
about what happened on the playground yesterday.
Julie, 9, Rochester, N.Y.

Mom still keeps her baby blanket under her pillow.
Well, I mean what's left of it. I guess that's sweet.

Naomi, 10, Philadelphia, Pa.

❧

My father's never barefoot. He'll walk around in
underwear, but he'll have sneakers on. Even in the
swimming pool, he wears flippers or pool shoes. He
sleeps with socks on. I've never seen his toes.

Gary, 14, Niles, Ill.

❧

Dad never throws out anything. He still has everything
he's ever owned, magazines, junk mail. Drawers full of
socks without elastic. Tests from grade school.

Mike, 13, Syracuse, N.Y.

Dad wears cowboy boots so he'll look taller.
Lauren, 7, Atlanta, Ga.

❦

They have dirty movies in their nightstands. XXX.
Howard, 17, Detroit, Mich.

❦

Dad slurps. Coffee, soup, wine. Milk. Ice cream.
Spaghetti sauce. His own spit.
Lee, 11, Napa, Calif.

❦

Whenever I get a phone call, "Who was it?
What did they want?" I get interrogated.
Paula, 13, Memphis, Tenn.

When company comes, they say grace.
That's the only time.
Phoebe, 18, Richmond, Va.

ⵦ

Mom talks to the bird. She tells it her troubles. Her
political views. Her concerns about the environment.
I mean, she's not goofing around, she *talks* to the bird.
Miriam, 13, Peoria, Ill.

ⵦ

Mom sings to the dog.
The dog can't stand it; he walks away.
Amber, 15, St. Louis, Mo.

My mom talks to herself. Out loud, I mean.
And she answers herself, too.
Meredith, 10, Washington, D.C.

❧

Mom never gets dirty jokes. She just doesn't.
Faye, 17, Boston, Mass.

❧

Mom can't tell a joke. She ruins them.
She forgets the punch line, or cracks up laughing
so she can't finish. Or she gives the punch line
as part of the set-up. It's pathetic.
Dierdre, 16, New York, N.Y.

Mom can't make decisions, even tiny little ones.
Like what to wear. Anyplace she has to go, she asks me
what to wear, if she has on too much makeup. Which
earrings. If, maybe, she should change her shoes. Then
she starts with my dad, asks him the same things.

Susan, 15, Lake Geneva, Wis.

෴

If my mom doesn't like somebody, she flatters them
and smiles a lot to cover up how she feels. Dad
probably doesn't remember if he likes somebody
or not until Mom tells him.

Ted, 14, Tulsa, Okla.

෴

They always act like I can't keep a secret. They never
tell me anything, all because a few years ago I forgot it
was a surprise and asked Gramma what she was going
to wear to her party.

Clay, 12, Irvine, Calif.

Mom and Dad had me before they were married.
I was actually the flower girl at their wedding. I don't
remember, but I've seen the pictures.

Theresa, 14, Phoenix, Ariz.

❧

I'm adopted, but I'm not supposed to tell anyone.

Abbey, 13, Bryn Mawr, Pa.

❧

My mom had her breasts enlarged.

Heather, 16, Ft. Lauderdale, Fla.

❧

Mom's jewelry's fake. Even the engagement ring.

Phil, 19, Baltimore, Md.

I know the smell of marijuana. Every so often, it comes
out of their bedroom. Then they giggle and raid the
refrigerator. I think I should discuss this with them,
but I don't know quite how to bring it up.

Trish, 17, Boston, Mass.

❧

Mom swears she wears a size seven shoe. But I
wear a seven and her shoes fall off my feet.
The boxes say eight and a half.

Miranda, 16, Washington, D.C.

❧

Dad's feet smell. If he takes off his shoes, you have to
leave. And he gets *so* insulted if you mention it.

Regina, 13, Toledo, Ohio

Mom sneaks cigarettes. She pretends she doesn't smoke,
and she made me swear never to tell my grandma.
Ellen, 10, Topeka, Kans.

⁂

They speak German when they don't want us to
understand. I didn't even know it was a different
language until I was maybe seven or eight and a friend
was over. My friend asked what language my parents
were speaking. I'd just assumed it was English.
I mean, I understood every word.
Gail, 17, Minneapolis, Minn.

⁂

In the middle of dinner, my dad'll say, "WHO PASSED
GAS?" Or "WHO CUT THE CHEESE?" He'll start
belching contests with my brothers.
Sherry, 14, Davenport, Iowa

CHAPTER 5

Happy Days

For some, it almost always involves a ball. For others, glitter and glue. For most kids, though, fun can be found almost anywhere, using anything.

That is, until their parents get involved. After that, it becomes clear that "fun," like beauty, is in the eyes of the beholder; Mom's fun might well be Junior's hell.

"My mother loves going to the mall," says Trevor, ten. "She'd spend her life there, if she could. Believe me, you don't want to go there with her. You never know *when* you'll get back."

No matter how they define fun, most families find limited opportunity to pursue it. Many well-intentioned parents cope by scheduling, orchestrating, and preplan-

133

ning. They fill children's spare time with lessons, classes, troops, and teams; arrange outings in campers, cabins, condos, and cruise ships. And, whatever the agenda, however hurried or harried they become, they remain resolute that their families *will* enjoy themselves.

Other parents, exhausted by the pressures of daily life, use free time to recuperate, relax, and collapse. The children, they assume, will find their own entertainment; they just hope it'll be quiet.

No matter what their families do for fun, though, most kids value the time they spend together. Even those who criticize the specifics prize the shared moments. And, in time, they'll probably prize them even more. After all, today's scrambled Saturdays, hellish hobbies, and awful outings are destined to become the heart of tomorrow's Good Old Days.

❧

My favorite thing is when we make cookies and then we get to scrape the bowl. Even though Mom licks most of the batter, even right off my fingers.

Jillian, 8, Stamford, Conn.

For Mom, fun is shopping sprees. She, like, gets high by
spending money. Buying things cheers her up, makes
her giddy. They can last hours. "Here—try this on.
What a *bargain*! Isn't this fun?"
Andy, 14, St. Louis, Mo.

They videotape everything. Not just TV shows off the
air. But everything we do. Smile. Turn around. Wave.
Blow me a kiss. No, not like that—act natural!
Robin, 11, Des Moines, Iowa

On car trips, they argue the whole way. About if Dad's
speeding, about the map, about being behind schedule.
We're not allowed to ask how much longer till we get
there. Or if we can stop to go to the bathroom.
Carly, 10, Cherry Hill, N.J.

We've been to Disney World four times. I'd really like to go someplace else, but Dad says it's the best deal. The place is clean and you know what you're getting for your money.

Mike, 13, Syracuse, N.Y.

❧

Mom's the navigator on trips. She'll tell you where to turn eighty-three times, what lane to get into four miles before the turn, when to put on your signal about two miles before the turn, and then, when it's time to turn and you're in the left turn only lane, she says, "No, it's not this corner, it must be the next one," or "I meant *that* corner," or "I meant turn *right*." It's never her fault, either. You heard her wrong. You weren't paying attention.

Alan, 17, Munster, Ind.

For our family, vacations have to be learning experiences. We've gone to remote areas of the Yucatan, the rain forest in South America, safari in Africa, camping in the Sahara. We've had every kind of inoculation, and we've never, as far as I can remember, gone anywhere we can drink the water. Other kids get to go to, like, Disney World or Club Med. Places with room service. Places with plumbing.

Sandy, 19, Rochester, N.Y.

⚬

My dad loves family projects. He buys wood and tools and we have to help him make stuff. Like the bird house, and the tree house. He measures and saws and we have to stand around holding tools.

Ariel, 9, Merion, Pa.

We play the road kill game. On the road, we count
dead animals, see who spots the most.

Jane, 10, Pittsburgh, Pa.

❧

Dad loves the outdoors. We have tents and sleeping
bags and hiking boots and gear. We trek through buggy,
muddy woods. I have to camp out with mosquitoes,
ants, snakes, poison oak, my sisters, and my allergies.
And you have to take leaks in the woods. If it rains,
the fire goes out and the tent caves in. Nobody has fun
except Dad. He thinks it's great.

Ken, 11, Amherst, N.Y.

❧

It takes my dad half an hour to set up a camera shot.
You have to hold still while he gets the focus
and the composition and the angle and then he
rearranges everybody. By the time he's ready to shoot,
you're ready to smash his camera.

Donald, 10, Harrisburg, Pa.

My mom's afraid of being up high.
So we aren't allowed to climb monkey bars or go on
ferris wheels. Sometimes she gives me a hard
time about swinging too high.

Debbie, 8, Cincinnati, Ohio

☙

Mom's phobic about airplanes, so we all fly
together or nobody flies. That way there'll be no
survivors. When we flew to Florida,
she drank vodka the whole way.

Flora, 13, New York, N.Y.

☙

When we go anywhere, Dad's like,
"Don't bother me, I'm on vacation. The only thing
I'm gonna do all week is roll over."

Doug, 12, Chicago, Ill.

When we travel or go anywhere, all you hear about
afterwards is the food. If someone asks, "How was
Guatemala?" Dad'll say, "Fantastic omelets. Fabulous
lobster. But you have to wait hours for service."
All they talk about is what was served, how it tasted,
how much it cost, how it looked. Presentation counts.
You can't just have poached salmon. Needs to
be displayed well, served pretty.

Deirdre, 16, New York, N.Y.

My mother will not go into any natural body of water.
It's not clean. There are things living in there. Even
with chlorine at a swimming pool, she keeps her head
above the water. She never ever submerges her face or
gets her hair wet. She gets upset if you splash.

Lisa, 13, Salt Lake City, Utah

Do not go canoeing with my mother.

Pete, 13, Evanston, Ill.

Dad loves to take us fishing. I get seasick and then
they filet the things all over the deck. Everything's slimy
and slippery and smells of fish blood. Dad has a
great time. We bring home a bunch of fish pieces and
Mom actually expects us to eat it.
Marty, 11, Newcastle, Del.

❧

On vacations, when we stay in motels,
they make me stay in the same bed as my little brother.
I'm afraid I'll get warts.
Mandy, 9, Winston-Salem, N.C.

❧

Every year, we go to visit our cousins in North
Carolina. There's nothing to do there but snap green
beans. For fun, we sit around the barber shop and
watch the hair pile up. Or shoot tin cans.
JB, 11, Philadelphia, Pa.

My parents' greatest enjoyment isn't doing stuff,
it's deciding what stuff to do. They never actually buy
anything until they've spent weeks comparing prices
from every possible store. They never go out to dinner
until they've considered every possible restaurant,
its pros and cons regarding service, crowds, quality of
food. Forget planning vacations. By the time they
actually evaluate every possible destination,
it's too late to get reservations.

Max, 16, Miami, Fla.

❧

Whenever we go somewhere in the car,
Mom reads signs out loud. Exit ramp numbers,
billboards, traffic directions, whatever.

Beth, 15, Atlanta, Ga.

❧

Dad won't stop except for gas. They bring a training
potty in case you have to go or throw up.

Rick, 9, Narberth, Pa.

This is what vacations are like. You have to get up while it's still dark and get stuffed in the back seat with both your brothers and all their games, so any way you move one of them yells at you and you always have somebody's elbows or feet in your face.

Audrey, 7, Baltimore, Md.

They don't want to waste any time on a trip. So we go
real early and don't come home till real late. And every
minute is planned. You have to stick to the agenda, see
this, do that, take pictures of everything. It's amazing
when you get the pictures. "What's this, Dad? The
Hoover Dam?" None of us can remember being there.

Janice, 14, Sarasota, Fla.

❧

Dad spends a lot of time planning our trips,
and we have to stick to his plan. If he's planned to ski
and there's no snow, we ski on dirt. If it's cold and
he's planned a beach day, we go to the beach
and freeze. If he's planned to bring cold drinks,
we drink cold drinks, even if our teeth are chattering.
You have to do it: It's part of the plan.

Dave, 12, Dayton, Ohio

I have to share their motel room.
They keep the TV on real late, and Dad snores.
Jaye, 10, New Orleans, La.

❦

Mom sings oldies in the car. She wants us
to sing with her and do hand motions.
Alex, 9, Bridgewater, N.J.

❦

On trips, they like to visit graveyards and
read the headstones of dead people. "Look at this,
Andy! A whole family—seven kids—died the
same year! And one of them was only a year old!"
Like, Mom? Is this supposed to be fun?
Andrea, 13, Chevy Chase, Md.

When my dad's in his chair, he's in his chair.
He's happy there. And nothing, certainly not a measly
doorbell, phone, fire, or child is going to get him out.
Nate, 16, Evanston, Ill.

❧

They play duets on their recorders.
Ashley, 14, Boca Raton, Fla.

❧

Sunday mornings, my father sings Frank Sinatra songs.
He also sings them in the shower. My mom does
Johnny Mathis. *She* can almost carry the tune.
Andy, 12, Detroit, Mich.

❧

All they ever do is watch TV.
So the only thing we do together is watch TV.
Vanessa, 15, Boston, Mass.

Dad changes channels right in the middle
of a show. If he's in the room, you never find out
what a show's about. It's like television salad,
a little of everything, tossed together.
Gabe, 12, Villanova, Pa.

I'm watching TV, and Dad walks in and turns it off,
right in the middle of a show. "Enough TV," he'll say.
Then he'll walk out, leaving me sitting there.
Desmond, 9, Selma, Ala.

When we watch TV, they make the same predictable
comments and have the same predictable reactions.
"He's so funny!" Or, "I can't stand that guy." "I *hate*
this commercial!" Whenever that funniest home videos
show comes on, my dad tells the host, "Shut up, Bob."
Steve, 13, Framingham, Mass.

My mom loves to discuss people she doesn't even know. Movie stars, TV actors. She worries about whether Oprah will ever have a baby. She has opinions about Whitney Houston's marriage. She doesn't like Jason Alexander, that guy who plays George on *Seinfeld*, because "He's too good at that part. He must really be that way." These are total strangers, but she has her opinions.

Heather, 16, Ft. Lauderdale, Fla.

❧

Mom likes me to watch her soaps with her. She tapes them while she's at work so we can watch them at night. She knows each character like a friend.

Nina, 16, Cicero, Ill.

❧

They're Trekkies.

Carson, 17, Des Moines, Iowa

They rent movies for us to watch together. They love
bad horror movies. To them, worse is better.
They love the kind with spaceships made from soup
cans, where you can see the strings holding them up.
Myra, 12, Birmingham, Ala.

Dad yells at news anchors, argues with commentators.
When political ads come on, he shouts at the narrators.
You can't ever hear the television.
Ben, 13, Dallas, Tex.

When Dad and I watch sports, he curses the
coaches, refs, umpires, quarterbacks, pitchers.
He's on his feet, waving his arms, cursing
and hollering as if he owns the team.
Bobby, 14, Houston, Tex.

Dad's favorite thing is sleeping. He dozes off anywhere.
At the movies. In church. At my sister's ballet recital. At
parties. He finds a comfortable chair and Zs out. If you
want to find him, you listen for the snores.
Jessie, 14, Detroit, Mich.

❦

Dad has certain stories he likes to tell.
The same ones, again and again. You know where
he's going from the first word. You think, here we go
again ... the one about great-grandma's yellow
raisins or great-grandpa's hearing aid.
Alan, 16, Shreveport, La.

❦

Dad loves his cigars.
Mitch, 10, Newark, Del.

Dad wiggles ears. He thinks it's fun.
He also wiggles his scalp.
Monica, 8, Highland Park, Ill.

Whatever happens to me, my dad has to relate it to
some memory from his own childhood. If I go to camp,
get a zit, go to a dance, win a game, get a low grade
or a high grade, break my arm, get in a fight.
Whatever. He likes to talk about his past, and he
assumes everyone likes to listen.
Neil, 13, Boulder, Colo.

Dad is serious about his reading. And Mom's
favorite thing is to soak in the tub. I mean, the house
could burn, but they wouldn't notice till the
chapter was done or the water got cold.
Chuck, 14, Toledo, Ohio

When they go out, I have to go with them. They don't want to let me stay by myself, and I'm too old for a babysitter. So I have to go to all these dinners and places with grownups, and they make me wear a suit.

Dylan, 10, Providence, R.I.

❧

Dad *loves* to make jokes, even at other people's expense. When I was little, he told me a watermelon would grow in my stomach if I swallowed a seed. I believed him, wouldn't eat watermelon till I was like eleven.

Trish, 14, Kenosha, Wis.

❧

Whenever we go out to dinner, Dad orders a drink with a maraschino cherry and ties the stem in a knot with his tongue. He's quite proud of this skill. He has us time him, to see how fast he can do it.

Nora, 9, Wilmette, Ill.

Dad serves mashed potatoes by
flinging them out of the spoon and hoping they
land on your plate. They usually do.
Ned, 9, Philadelphia, Pa.

Dad truly believes he can play the violin.
Sarah, 15, Minneapolis, Minn.

❧

Dad does dialects and imitations. Sometimes
he'll stay in character for days. His Seinfeld's not bad.
His Bogart's weak. And his Cary Grant's awful.
When he does George Jefferson, he calls my
mom "Wheezy" all night.
Nate, 16, Evanston, Ill.

❧

Dad sings duets with our dog.
Chris, 14, Sonoma, Calif.

❧

We'll play gin, but we've got to let my
dad win or he'll sulk.
Ned, 16, Portland, Oreg.

On Sunday mornings, Daddy just won't get up. So, finally, we all pull him out of bed. He pretends he's asleep but he's not really, and we climb on him and pull his feet. He pretends to get mad.

Well, I *think* he's pretending.

Gabrielle, 7, Brooklyn, N.Y.

❧

Whenever they go to a dinner or a party, the whole next day my dad goes, "I was the best looking guy there, wasn't I, Honey?" Or, "Yours truly had the best head of hair there!"

Jeff, 14, Skokie, Ill.

❧

Dad loves his cars. He has a picture of every car he's ever owned. He has them mostly in albums, but some are in frames. Hung up, in the family room on the wall. He has stories about each one. It's like they're his relatives. Or girlfriends.

Matt, 14, Randolph, Vt.

To my dad, fun is going to car dealerships to shop around. He likes the smell of new cars. He doesn't need to buy them, he just sits in them and breathes. And anything you say, he relates it to cars. If I tell him, "Dad, I went to a ball game with Elliot last night," he'll say, "Yeah? What kind of car did you ride in?"

Craig, 15, Richmond, Va.

❧

My dad loves geography. His favorite thing is to take us to a map and show us every place he's ever been or where grandma was born or where great-grandfather served in WWI.

Ronald, 14, St. Paul, Minn.

❧

Dad will always get cheered up by a good belching contest.

Samantha, 9, Manchester, N.H.

Farts are all my father ever talks about.
Or variations on farts. Cutting cheese, blowing wind,
passing gas. He has a million fart jokes.
Bill, 12, Kansas City, Mo.

❧

Dad likes anything gross. Whoopie
cushions. Booger jokes, throw-up jokes,
diarrhea jokes. Anything disgusting.
Rick, 8, Taos, N.Mex.

❧

To make a point, my father quotes literature. Like
Shakespeare. In an English accent, like he's on stage.
"The rain it raineth every day..." Like that.
Phil, 19, Baltimore, Md.

You can't just tell my dad how to play a game.
He has to read the rules for himself. Usually out loud.
All the rules, even the exceptions.

Marta, 11, Pittsburgh, Pa.

❧

Dad's so competitive. It doesn't matter what the game
is. Hearts, monopoly. Parcheesi. Dad says, "Prepare to
die." Or, "Any last words?" He shows no mercy, even
to my sister, who's only like seven years old. Then he
gloats, like he's proud he could beat a couple of kids.

Blair, 13, Washington, D.C.

❧

My dad loves toys. He buys "me" stuff.
Automatic water guns, a pool table, computer
games, a Skidoo. Then he plays with them.

Casey, 15, Amherst, Mass.

They want to do whatever kids do. Rollerblade, ride
bikes, skateboard. They like street hockey.
Whatever the kids on the street want to play,
my mom and dad tag along.
Ricky, 10, Narberth, Pa.

∽

Dad likes me to go on-line with him. But you can't
really do that together. Basically, I sit there
and watch Dad go on-line.
Sydney, 13, San Diego, Calif.

∽

I have to play cards with Grandma.
This is my job in the family.
Amy, 8, Phoenix, Ariz.

We have to do jigsaw puzzles. They're all over
the family room floor. We never finish any, and,
actually, the pieces are all mixed up.
Brendon, 12, St. Paul, Minn.

When they play bridge, which is every weekend,
you think they're going to kill each other.
This is what they do for *fun*.
Bev, 17, Chicago, Ill.

They *love* flea markets. They're always looking through
piles of junk. We drive for miles, hours. And then, if
they find something, like a table or cabinet, my brother
and I have to sit on top of each other to fit it in the car.
Glen, 10, Chevy Chase, Md.

They read junk mail. "You never know when you'll
get something valuable," they say.
Valerie, 14, Milwaukee, Wis.

Trivia is my parents' favorite activity.
Except for charades.
Luke, 15, Los Angeles, Calif.

Catastrophes fascinate my mom. She'll tell you about
anyone who's died, had a heart attack or operation.
Plane crashes, terrorist acts, unsolved murders.
Whose sister's cousin's ex-wife has cancer. Who got
fired. Whose brother-in-law's father-in-law had a car
accident after abandoning his pregnant third wife.
Dinner's like a soap opera summary.
Diane, 17, Raleigh, N.C.

My mom knits. She grinds her teeth
and jabs needles. Scary.
Stephanie, 14, Cherry Hill, N.J.

❧

All they really like to do is eat. Everything's about
where we should eat, what's for dinner, should we have
a snack? If you don't want a marshmallow sundae,
they think something's wrong with you.
Liz, 15, New Orleans, La.

❧

"Please Don't Kiss Me
at the Bus Stop!"
164

Mom's into health foods. We're all on vegetarian,
fat-free diets now. No ice cream or chocolate. If I want
a burger, I have to sneak to the neighbors'.
Tom, 15, Madison, Wis.

They spend hours clipping coupons, discussing the
savings. "Six dollars this week!" They're ecstatic.
Cindy, 16, Buffalo, N.Y.

They discuss recipes from food magazines. And coffee
is the subject they talk about the most. Except, maybe,
wine. They have debates about wine. You'd think
the world revolved around their cuisine.
Brad, 17, Atlanta, Ga.

I think they really like to worry. Like they read the
labels from food packages out loud and worry about
the chemical additives. They read articles in the
newspaper about drive-by shootings or some new
virus and they worry about that. Weekends, they sit
around and talk about what might happen if...
Pick a topic, they'll worry about it.
Leon, 19, Washington, D.C.

Mom brags. This is her favorite activity.
Telling people how wonderful we all are in school,
how well my father's career is going, how she just
got a raise at work, how perfect everything is,
how nothing could be better.

Maggie, 11, Dallas, Tex.

❧

Mom loves to have people over. She invites
people all the time, doesn't think about it.
You never know who's showing up for dinner.
Well, half the time, *she* doesn't, either.

Amy, 14, St. Louis, Mo.

❧

Mom likes talking on the phone. All day. She does
everything while she's on the phone. Cook, eat, take a
bath, wash dishes, pay bills, exercise. The only thing
she doesn't do on the phone, probably, is sleep.

Rebecca, 9, St. Charles, Ill.

My mom whistles along when I practice piano. If I get
stuck, she keeps on going and gets ahead of me,
so then I have to race to catch up. Or, sometimes,
if I make a mistake, she keeps on whistling the same
note over and over again until I get it right.

Esta, 14, Glenview, Ill.

❧

I like computer games, but they say, "You're going to
go blind if you sit there any more." Or, "Why don't
you go play outside?" They'd rather have me hang out
on the streets than sit at the computer.

Jason, 10, Philadelphia, Pa.

❧

We go the symphony. Dad falls asleep and
I'm pretty bored. But it's culture.

Kate, 10, Chicago, Ill.

They like to put my doll's clothes on the dog.
She looks cute in them.
Lisa, 8, Munster, Ind.

❧

Mom gets mad if the dog gets wet or muddy. She wants
me to put booties on him when he goes outside.
Curt, 10, New York, N.Y.

❧

They never do anything for fun. They're too busy.
I don't know what they're doing, they're just busy.
Ask them to do something. You'll see. They'll say,
"Not now. We're busy."
Burke, 12, Memphis, Tenn.

Dad's always working or on the phone. The only time
you can get his attention is when he says,
"Quiet. I'm on the phone." And Mom has no time
for fun; she has lists of chores to do. "Fix the faucet,
plant the bulbs, clean the closets." Trust me,
"Party, party!" is not on her list.

Jen, 11, Denver, Colo.

Family Values

Whether they spout the Golden Rule or sport golden Rolexes, all parents are role models for their children. Every day of the year, morning till night, through every word and deed, Moms and Dads teach their offspring the hows, whys, and wherefores of life.

And children, observant tykes that they are, don't miss a syllable, facial expression, or gesture. They pick up their parents' messages, both intentional and accidental, and impose meaning on them. Inadvertent actions transform into lessons; specific incidents evolve into generalized truths; random observations lead to radical conclusions. And no contradiction goes unnoticed.

171

"How can they get mad when I budge in front of my brother?" says Roger, ten. "I mean, you should see my dad cut in on the highway. Or Mom at the mall—she can beat out *anybody* when she sees something good on sale."

Even parents who recite traditional values of baseball, apple pie, and the American flag give off other, nonverbal, and, often, unintentional signals about what's important, what's not, what's cool, what's hot. From materialism to spiritualism, finances to family ties, kids learn as much from casual observation as from careful explanation.

Pam, seven, gives an example. "Dad says *I* should save my allowance instead of shopping. But *he* uses credit cards. If he'd give me a credit card, I could buy things without money, same as him."

❧

I don't want to hurt their feelings. But, like, Santa? I know it's really all just pretend and made up, isn't it?

Laurie, 6, St. Cloud, Minn.

On Christmas, you can't walk through our house.
There's crumpled wrapping paper everywhere.
You can't see the furniture. There's piles of paper and
ribbon up to the ceiling. The kids all jump in it, and
squunch it into balls and have fights with it. We build
forts with the boxes. It takes a while to find the
presents. They get lost underneath.

Brooke, 12, Indianapolis, Ind.

☙

They think they fool us. They think we don't know
about the Santa thing. Oh, come on. We even know
where the stuff is stashed and what it is.

Greg, 7, Narberth, Pa.

☙

Mom can't stand it. She always tells us what we're
getting. And we always open our presents on Christmas
Eve; she can't wait till the morning. Same with birthdays.
She gives us the cake and presents the night before.

Lynne, 11, Concord, N.H.

We never had a Tooth Fairy. I never heard of it till I
was, maybe, ten or twelve. Dad just yanked our teeth if
they got too loose. And that was the end.

James, 14, Topeka, Kans.

❧

We have certain routines that no one ever breaks.
Every Sunday morning, Dad listens to opera.
Every Fourth of July, we eat hotdogs and potato salad
and Dad sets off firecrackers. Rain or shine, we spend
Memorial Day where Dad grew up, near the ocean.
Christmas, no matter how much we complain
about it, is at Aunt Lil's.

Mandy, 14, Winston-Salem, N.C.

❧

"Please Don't Kiss Me
at the Bus Stop!"

174

Every year, we have to get new and better Christmas
decorations. It's like we have to outdo not just the
neighbors, but also ourselves from the year before.

Rob, 12, Glenview, Ill.

We aren't Christian, but Mom and Dad don't want
us to feel left out, so we get a tree anyway. But we
aren't allowed to tell Grandma.
Sam, 9, Huntingdon Valley, Pa.

⚜

Every year, they complain about Christmas.
How ridiculous it's become, how much it costs, what
a pain it is sending cards, how many people they have
to buy presents for. But every year, they invite more
people over, give more gifts, spend more money.
And they make us go caroling.
Bob, 15, Richmond, Va.

⚜

Christmas and Easter, Mom makes me dress like
my little sister. She buys us two of the same.
Margaret, 9, Lexington, Va.

Mom insists on making our Halloween costumes. Uh.
Nobody ever knows what we are.

Bonnie, 10, Brooklyn, N.Y.

❧

We have to have a haunted house in our basement
every Halloween. Dad loves to hide in the closet and
jump out with a flashlight under his face. He puts fake
spider webs in his hair. He wraps us up like mummies
and we lie in the dark waiting for trick or treaters to
come by so we can sit up and go, "BOO!"

Keith, 10, Wilmington, Del.

❧

On Halloween, they dress in costumes. Like kids. They
actually scare preschoolers.

Louise, 12, Brookline, Mass.

We're the family that doesn't give out candy on Halloween. We give out "healthy snacks," like apples and raisins.

Germaine, 14, Philadelphia, Pa.

They never really explained to us about holidays so, when I was little, I used to think that the holidays were about the *food*. Turkey and apple pie were why you celebrated Thanksgiving. Matzo and chicken soup were Passover. Gifts and potato pancakes with applesauce were the reason for Hanukkah.

Naomi, 17, Highland Park, Ill.

We have two religions. Mom and Dad can't agree what to be. So sometimes we go to church, sometimes synagogue. They argue about whether I'll have a Bar Mitzvah. But it's not so bad—I get Hanukkah *and* Christmas presents.

Mike, 9, New York, N.Y.

Every year, all our cousins bring a dish for Thanksgiving dinner. One brings pies, another brings candied sweet potatoes. Cousin Gladys always brings stringbeans. Well, once she brought broccoli. My mom says Gladys never spends more than five dollars.

Mimi, 15, Normal, Ill.

❧

We have the same menu every Thanksgiving. One year, Mom made a new stuffing for the turkey. There was almost a riot, and Aunt Reggie got insulted that her usual recipe wasn't used. "What, nobody likes *my* stuffing? All these years, you've *pretended* to like it?" There was a confrontation; believe me, it wasn't pretty.

Howard, 14, Denver, Colo.

Every year, my mom makes brownies for
Thanksgiving and we have to hide them, because all
my cousins steal them from the kitchen before dinner
and hardly any are left for dessert.

Randy, 12, Dallas, Tex.

❧

Every Thanksgiving, Mom calls Grandma in Florida.
There are about sixteen kids, all the cousins,
and our moms and dads. And everybody's running
around until Mom grabs them and sticks the
phone in their ear. Grandma says, "Who's this? Who?
How are you, Darling? I love you. Who else is there?
Let me talk to the next one."

Liz, 12, Marblehead, Mass.

Aunt Ida *has* to cook the turkey. This irritates my mom. "Why does Ida always have to do the turkey? Isn't *my* turkey good enough?" Then, what's with the carving? Is this some kind of macho thing? Is this only in our family? Dad says, "Why does Steve carve every year? Because he's a doctor? Do you have to be a surgeon?"

Wendy, 14, St. Louis, Mo.

❧

My mom makes my sister and me set the table for company. Then she tells everybody that we set it, and they all go, "Oh what a beautiful table you set!" like putting plates out is a major accomplishment.

Heather, 16, Ft. Lauderdale, Fla.

❧

Dad counts the silver after people leave. Once we were missing a teaspoon. We had to search the garbage until he discovered he'd counted wrong. At least he didn't make us follow people home and search their pockets.

Denise, 12, Baltimore, Md.

When we have people over, Mom tells me to put the
platters out, then she comes out and rearranges them.
She'll move the cheese and crackers two inches to
the right, the clam dip half an inch to the left.
Like I did it wrong or something.
Julia, 15, Tacoma, Wash.

Mom gets furious that my aunts take all the
leftovers. They just go into the kitchen and pack up
stuff. She tells my sister and me to hide whatever
we want and save it in the back of the fridge,
behind the old jars of pickles.
Dena, 9, Manchester, N.H.

I'm fifteen, and whenever we have company,
I have to sit with the little kids.
Ned, 15, Washington, D.C.

I have to sit at the kids' table even though I'm nineteen. When I complain, my parents tell me to forget it. Mom didn't move up until Uncle Jack died, so there was a vacancy. By then she was married, almost thirty.

Candace, 19, Oklahoma City, Okla.

They make me play with my cousins even
though they're girls. If I ask why I have to,
Mom says, "They're your cousins."

Kevin, 8, Little Rock, Ark.

Every year Mom says the holidays aren't going to be at
our house, when she knows very well that nobody else
is going to do it, so then she waits till the last minute
and it's a frantic rush to get everything together. She
can't just plan it. Makes us all crazy.

Chuck, 11, Southfield, Mich.

Every year, the kids put on plays. We have a script
and costumes and makeup. I'm the youngest,
so I always have to be a turkey on Thanksgiving.
And the donkey on Christmas.

Joy, 9, Atlanta, Ga.

Family Values

183

Every holiday, my parents make me write a poem
to read before dinner, in honor of the event.
Or they ask me to read my poetry to company.
They say my poems are a tradition.
Molly, 14, Des Moines, Iowa

∝

Every holiday, we have to suffer through Uncle Ralph's
stories and jokes, Uncle Joe's cigars, Aunt Sonia's wet
kisses, Aunt Minnie's horrible perfume. We have to let
the twins mess up our rooms and play with our stuff.
If we complain, Mom and Dad say, "Put up with it.
They're your family. It's only for a day."
Barbara, 16, Baton Rouge, La.

∝

My family takes longer to say goodbye than they
spend visiting at an entire occasion. They have to say
goodbye personally, to each relative individually, and
there are usually about fifty of them there.
Cindy, 17, Chicago, Ill.

When we have company and there might not be
enough for seconds, Mom has a signal to tell us
"family, hold back." She says, "Is it too warm
in here?" and scratches her nose.
Karen, 10, Peoria, Ill.

∽

When Dad's family comes over, Mom says they eat
everything in sight, so she only puts half of it out, and
puts the rest away. "It's too good for them," she says.
Monica, 10, Bronx, N.Y.

∽

At ballgames or the Fourth of July, Dad doesn't just
sing the national anthem, he stands at attention and
salutes the flag. He was a Coast Guard officer, maybe
twenty years ago. He flies the flag whenever he's home.
Has us do morning and evening colors with him.
Lloyd, 12, Memphis, Tenn.

Every weekend, unless it's raining or blizzarding,
Dad hangs the American flag in our yard. Like why?
So maybe everybody in the neighborhood will
know what country they're in?
Don, 15, Fort Wayne, Ind.

☙

Every year, we go to the shore and Dad
"falls" into the bay. In his clothes. Every year.
He starts the season that way.
Dwayne, 17, Newark, Del.

☙

For their twenty-fifth anniversary, my parents said,
"Don't give us a party." We said, okay, we wouldn't.
They pouted for weeks. So we gave them a surprise
party. They had a ball. But they scolded us, "Why'd
you do that? We *said* we didn't want a party.
Now you've wasted all that money."
Sophie, 18, Buffalo, N.Y.

On birthdays, the rule is that you can't talk
after you blow out candles until you eat *all* your cake.
So, every year, my dad tries to get you to talk.
He asks you questions, tries to trick you. He thinks
it's a scream if you fall for it. "Here, Lizzie,"
he'll say, "phone for you."

Liz, 12, Tuscaloosa, Ala.

❧

Every birthday, my mom talks about how
strange it is to get old; how she's surprised every
time she looks in the mirror to see that she's not
nineteen; how, sooner or later, everybody gets
something fatal or debilitating; how, in the
long run, nobody wins the game of life.

Nan, 18, Corpus Christi, Tex.

Family Values

Being happy depresses my mom; she thinks it's asking for trouble. She gets nervous if things are going too well. "If things are up," she says, "they can only go down." Her attitude is that everything will eventually be over, so why enjoy it? Why set yourself up for a loss? The only emotion she trusts is melancholy.

Susan, 19, Madison, Wis.

❧

Mom's obsessed with death. Any occasion—New Year's, Christmas, her anniversary—*any* milestone's a sign that our lives are passing, that death is that much closer. At my brother's college graduation, she sighed, "Rotting flesh. We're going to be rotting flesh."

Josh, 20, Richmond, Va.

❧

Every night at dinner, my dad gives us math problems to solve. We aren't supposed to talk until we figure out the answers. And we can't convince him this isn't fun.

Michelle, 11, St. Paul, Minn.

They never compliment me. The best I get is,
"You did fine." Or, "You look okay." This is because
the Evil Eye is watching. If you point out something
good about a person, the Evil Eye will see and
bring them bad luck. I don't know why.
Brandy, 12, Concord, N.H.

⚬

My mom has angels, pennies, good
luck charms, crystals, medals.
Carries them with her, always, in her purse.
Audrey, 13, Reno, Nev.

⚬

There's nothing my mom won't do to
pick up a heads-up penny.
Sean, 9, Oakland, Calif.

I have to seriously talk to my dad for a half an
hour to get any money out of him. "Dad,
I need money for lunch." He'll say, "Didn't I
just give you lunch money *last* week?"

Marlee, 15, Orlando, Fla.

☙

I don't get my allowance unless I do my chores. If my
bed wasn't made *one* day, I'm out five dollars. The
only way I can make it back is by doing extra chores.
Like clean the garage. Or run the vacuum.

Neil, 13, Boulder, Colo.

☙

If I want extra money, they make me babysit
my maggoty little brother.

Maureen, 12, Albuquerque, N.Mex.

They have a hundred credit cards and never can find the one they're looking for. You can stand at a cash register for half an hour while they search. I don't think I've ever seen them pay with real money.

Frank, 11, Portland, Maine

❧

Mom lives for bargains. She brags to neighbors about getting half off on Dad's Jockeys. She gets excited about sales on *relish* and discusses the price with her friends. "Of course," she'll say, "you have to buy the economy size." Is this really important to her? I mean, if it is, I totally dread growing up.

Anne, 19, Santa Monica, Calif.

❧

They always forget to give me my allowance, and when I remind them, they insist they already gave it to me. It's like they think I'd cheat them and try to get it twice. Which isn't a bad idea, really.

Bob, 14, Boston, Mass.

Dad'll bet anybody about anything. How long until Mom gets off the phone. The number of times the newsman will say "hopefully" in a half-hour broadcast. How many telemarketing calls we get in a week. And he'll bet for any stakes. Technically, he now owns my little sisters' Barbie dolls.

Walt, 19, Erie, Pa.

❧

Dad's office bets on the football games every week. He gets totally nuts about it. If he misses the spread, things can get ugly. But if he wins, it's party time.

Paula, 13, Memphis, Tenn.

❧

Baseball's like my dad's religion. Lose or win. Dad's been a fan forever. Forget family or country. It's White Sox to the death.

Alicia, 10, Chicago, Ill.

You should hear the language they use.
Then they get surprised if we curse. "Young man,
where did you hear *that*?"
"Um. Right here?"
Craig, 11, Mount Lebanon, Pa.

❧

I mean, they're not, like, dangerous, but they're
definitely bigots. They hate just about everybody.
Or not hate. They just want them to get out of the
country and go live someplace far away.
Ray, 15, Miami, Fla.

❧

Mom marks passages in the Bible for us to read.
Amber, 10, Selma, Ala.

All of a sudden, my parents decided we were
going to keep Kosher. No more milk with dinner or
butter on your garlic bread. No more cheeseburgers.
If you put a plate in the wrong cabinet, it's all of a
sudden a crime. What? In restaurants, all we can
usually order is salad. Or pasta with oil.
Jeff, 11, Bala Cynwyd, Pa.

❧

They make me go to Sunday school even though
I told them God wasn't there. Well, He was there
one week, but He never came back.
Meredith, 6, Gladwyne, Pa.

❧

Every Sunday, we go to church. No excuses.
You have to get up, get dressed up, and go.
Dad says, if he has to, we have to.
Blake, 10, Tallahassee, Fla.

I have to go to Hebrew school. I can't stand it.
None of the kids can. My parents don't care. They say
that hating Hebrew school is part of the deal. They
hated it when they were kids, too.

Steve, 11, Cleveland, Ohio

❧

Every month, we spend a day at the cemetery,
visiting Grandmom and Grandpa and all our other
dead relatives. This is actually sort of dull.

Andy, 9, Jackson, Miss.

❧

We used to say prayers together every night.
Then Grandfather died, and Mom said she wasn't
talking to God anymore. She's mad at Him.
She said we can still pray, if we want to. But God'll
just have to understand; if my mom's mad at Him,
I'm not about to take sides against her.

Ward, 8, Corpus Christi, Tex.

They send us to Catholic school. They went
when they were kids. When Mom's mad at Dad,
she blames Catholic school for ruining him.
But they make us go anyway.
Christie, 9, Boston, Mass.

⁓

Mom says people judge you by your shoes.
Okay, fair enough. That's just another reason
why I want to wear my old sneaks.
Sean, 13, Syracuse, N.Y.

⁓

Mom insists that first impression is everything. After
five minutes, you'll never change anyone's mind about
you. So she doesn't want us to leave the house with a
single hair out of place. We have to stand up straight,
and our nails have to be perfectly clean, never chipped.
Kaye, 13, Washington, D.C.

They say it doesn't matter what "other people" do; we should do what we think is right. But *they* do what other people do. I mean, Dad can't stand suits, but he wears them every day. With *ties*. Why? Because he wants to do the same as everybody else at the office.

Paul, 14, New York, N.Y.

⌘

My mother never compromises or backs down. In a parking garage, she thought she'd been overcharged by three minutes, so she demanded to see the manager, even though it took like an hour to get him. He gave her a coupon for free parking, just to get rid of her. She tells people not just that she disagrees with them, but that they're wrong. Her nose puffs and she shouts her opinions about everything—politics, religion, education—whatever. My father tries to change the subject, or he retreats and waits for it to be over. Most people who know her just let her go on until she burns herself out.

Mort, 15, Memphis, Tenn.

You owe your blood relations first, your friends second.
Anybody else is basically on their own.

Mitch, 13, New York, N.Y.

❧

My father says that compromise is the key to success.
He says you should give in on small issues,
and always be prepared to give in 50 percent.
I actually applied this to my allowance. I asked him
for a ten dollar raise, knowing that, if I compromised
50 percent, I'd still get five. Of course, it didn't work.
He said I had no bargaining power.

Mort, 13, Ann Arbor, Mich.

❧

Mom says to assume people are lying to you, or at least
telling you things in a way that's favorable to them.
She's no exception. She'll say, "This'll just take
a second," when she stops at the mall. Or, "You'll
love it!" when she's just cut off all my hair.

Steve, 15, Des Moines, Iowa

They tell us that our family's like our team,
so we should root for each other and help each other
out no matter what. If one of us succeeds, we all
succeed. If one of us fails, we let ourselves and
the others down. If we fight among ourselves,
we're helping the opposition defeat us. It's us against
the world, all for one and one for all. Next they'll
get us uniforms, hold candlelight rallies.

Abby, 14, Albany, N.Y.

✺

We're not supposed to lie, right? Well, Dad told a
homeless guy he had no money on him, and I know he
did. He told me my drawing was "beautiful" when
I showed him scribble-scrabble. Mom told Aunt Celia,
"You've lost weight!" They lie, but only sometimes,
not all the time, so you never know.

Maggie, 9, Boston, Mass.

Mom takes in strays. We had nine cats last year.
Now there are seven. When I try to do my homework,
they always sit on my paper or book.
If I move one, another climbs on.
Clark, 9, Sioux City, Iowa

౸

My dad thinks every creature is special, so you can't
kill a spider. You have to chase it outside. Spiders. Flies.
Moths. You literally have to save ladybugs from the
swimming pool. He swats mosquitoes, though.
But, I guess there are exceptions for self-defense.
Ken, 11, Amherst, N.Y.

When I pick my courses, my dad says, "Why would you want to study *Romantic poetry*? How will *that* help you get a job? Take something practical, that you can *use*. What can you do with an *English* major?"

Stan, 18, Dallas, Tex.

∽

I want to study computer science, but my parents want me to get a liberal arts education—study philosophy and art history. They want me to "broaden my mind" and "learn to think." Excuse me? I mean, is there an exploding job market for "broad-minded liberal-arts-educated thinkers?"

Phil, 19, Grand Rapids, Mich.

∽

Dad won't let me touch his car. He goes, "Who touched my car? Look at this smudge!"

Dan, 17, Lincolnwood, Ill.

Mom drives an old wreck. She doesn't need to impress
anybody. She says cars are necessities that serve
a function, just like toilets. Nothing more, nothing less.
She says she doesn't need a fancy car any more
than she needs a fancy toilet.

Dave, 15, Dayton, Ohio

❧

Dad has to have the most expensive car. Like he'll
sulk if someone has a better model. We console
him about this, but he doesn't get that we're teasing.
He thinks we're commiserating.

Gary, 14, Niles, Ill.

❧

Mom prides herself on being thrifty. She will drive
around town for an hour and a half to pay bills in
person so that she can save thirty-two cents per stamp.
Never mind the mileage. Or the value of her time.

Melissa, 16, New Orleans, La.

Mom wants jewelry for every occasion. Don't bother getting her a sweater or perfume. Forget the flowers. She sits with her jewel box and says, "This was for my Sweet Sixteen. From Aunt Beth. This your father gave me on our first anniversary..."
Jade, 16, Baton Rouge, La.

~

Mom shops in thrift shops. She thinks it's great that she finds designer stuff cheap. I feel like things are crawling in my clothes. Or like I'm wearing stuff that belonged to some kid who died in a car crash. Or that I'll run into some kid at school and she'll say, "Hey, that's my old sweater!" It'll have her name in it, in indelible ink.
Marcy, 14, Chicago, Ill.

~

My uncles are mechanics. Dad's a contractor. They work with their hands, make fun of "college kids who don't like to get their hands dirty." In other words, me.
Bryan, 18, Baltimore, Md.

Dad went to Harvard and MIT. Mom went to
Columbia. My sister went to Yale. My older
brother went to Dartmouth. Phi Beta Kappa.
There's just a little bit of pressure on me.

Helene, 14, Evanston, Ill.

They make me write to the president. "It's your
world," they say. "You have to speak up." So I wrote
about whales and gorillas. And about the rainforest.
I don't know if the president even reads my letters.
I'm just a ten-year-old kid.

Nicholas, 10, Seattle, Wash.

My parents never walk. They drive everywhere. To the
drug store down the street. To the mailbox on the corner. My mom'll turn on the engine, just to use the car
phone. But she jogs every morning, to keep in shape.

Stacey, 15, Boulder, Colo.

They waste a lot. Leave the lights on,
the water running. If I say something to my dad
about this, he shouts, "I PAY FOR IT;
I CAN DO WHAT I DAMN WELL WANT!"
Brad, 11, Pittsburgh, Pa.

⁓

They're into conservation. Recycling. Composting.
The whole bit. They save the dog's poop.
Margo, 11, Bridgewater, N.J.

⁓

You don't want to get the hiccups around my daddy.
He won't give up until he scares them away.
Monica, 7, Highland Park, Ill.

We visit Grandpa every second Sunday. We sit there, and maybe he opens his eyes, but he has no clue why we're there. Sometimes we watch TV. We bring him food, like cake or cookies. Then we leave, and Mom says, "Well? How did he seem to you?"

Jane, 10, Pittsburgh, Pa.

Bumps in the Road

Inevitably, conflicts and upsets occur in even the happiest homes. Parents and children alike get irritable, sad, or angry from time to time. When they need to let off steam, most do so where it's safest: in the privacy and security of their own homes.

It is, therefore, in their own homes that most kids learn how to handle hostilities, mourn losses, manage conflicts, and express anger. Family outbursts and their outcomes become models for the rules of coping and fighting, even if those "rules" are never stated out loud.

"My parents," says Paul, twelve, "tell us that fighting's normal. They say it's the way people release tension. So, when they're mad, they just let it out. Then, five minutes after they're snarling like dogs, they're calling each other 'Snookie' and 'Bear,' like it never happened."

Kids say that spats and crises at home show that it's okay to express feelings. They see that life goes on after losses, relationships survive squabbles, love endures despite disagreements. Further, from what they witness at home, kids learn the limits of fair fighting. No matter how mad they get, they find that fists must never fly, that angry words can't be taken back, that broken promises can't be mended, and that the adage about sticks, stones, and broken bones is only partly true: Names can be hurtful weapons, too.

If I ever fight with other kids, Mom says I'm wrong.
I'm never allowed to fight or curse. If I'm mad,
I'm supposed to walk away, count to a hundred and
take deep breaths. As if she does that.
Bill, 9, Wichita, Kans.

I can tell when they're going to have a fight because
Mom says, "Donald, take the dog for a walk."
Donald, 9, San Francisco, Calif.

❧

My parents can fight over nothing. In the middle
of nothing. Then, when they're done, they tell us
never mind, it was nothing.
Jane, 10, Pittsburgh, Pa.

❧

When Mom gets mad, Dad asks her what's wrong.
She says, "You know very well what's wrong."
He says, "No, I don't."
She says, "Well, you should."
This goes on for a while, and Dad takes me aside and
asks me, "What's wrong with Mom?"
I say, "I don't know."
He says, "Yeah? Well, you should."
Heather, 16, Ft. Lauderdale, Fla.

When they argue, they don't listen to each other. They
go head to head and yell into each other's faces,
both at the same time. It's best to lie low and wait until
it passes. You just hope a fight doesn't start around
dinner time; it can be ten o'clock before we eat.

Mike, 13, Syracuse, N.Y.

❧

My parents interrupt each other and go off on tangents
so they end up arguing about what they're arguing
about. Like Mom'll say, "That's not the point."
Dad'll say, "Yes it is." She'll say, "It is not." He'll say,
"Well, then, what *is*?" And so on.

Dean, 14, Springfield, Mo.

❧

When Mom and Dad fight, they call each other names.
"Jerk." "Slimebucket." "A-hole." Real mature.

Peter, 11, Denver, Colo.

When they fight, they use the s-word. Even the f-word.
The d-word isn't nasty enough.
Melody, 11, Santa Fe, N.Mex.

⟡

They never argue in front of us kids. When we
leave the room, it starts; when we enter, it stops.
They're all smiles until we leave again. It's like
somebody turned the volume up and down and
then up again. Or switched channels.
Neil, 13, Boulder, Colo.

⟡

When I was little, sometimes Dad would warn me not to
go in the kitchen barefoot because 'Mommy broke some
glasses.' I knew that meant they'd had a fight and Mom
got so mad that she threw glasses at the walls. This never
happens anymore. Oh, she still throws stuff, but now
they get unbreakable tumblers and plastic cups.
Mandy, 14, Winston-Salem, N.C.

When they're fighting, they don't speak to each other.
They send messages through me. "Tell your father to
get his feet off the coffee table."
"Tell your mother I'll put my feet anywhere I damn
well want to." "Tell your father that if he won't
take his feet off the table, I'll come in there and
take them off for him."
They fight with each other, but they only talk to me.
I don't say a word.
Raymond, 14, Tulsa, Okla.

❧

Every so often, Dad'll warn me to watch out. Don't
breathe too loud. Mom's got PMS. She's on the warpath.
Jack, 13, Charlotte, N.C.

❧

When my mom's mad at him, Daddy asks me to find
out what's wrong. I think he's, like, scared of her.
Roz, 7, New Rochelle, N.Y.

I don't think my parents actually fight. At least, they don't fight in front of us kids. They don't have to, though. Because there's no point saying anything after Mom's eyebrow goes up.

Debbie, 8, Cincinnati, Ohio

%

My dad says, "Yes, Dear." Whatever my mom says, he says, "Yes, Dear." You know a big one's coming on; you can see her steaming. The more he says, "Yes, Dear," the more she steams.

Alexandra, 14, Chevy Chase, Md.

%

My dad has to yell a certain amount every day. He has to let off steam. You don't take it personally.

Rick, 9, Narberth, Pa.

They don't exactly fight; they bicker. Constantly.
Over nothing. When to turn on the windshield wipers.
Who left the lights on in the bathroom. Folding
the newspaper. Stuff like that.

Bryan, 18, Baltimore, Md.

❧

Mom never yells. She gives us "The Look."
I wish she would yell. It'd be easier to take.

Marissa, 14, Seattle, Wash.

❧

Mom doesn't complain. She doesn't get mad. She just
gets quiet. Sometimes, she doesn't speak for days.

Jade, 16, Baton Rouge, La.

When they're arguing, there's a lot of banging and
slamming. Drawers, doors, cabinets. Heads, maybe.
Andy, 14, St. Louis, Mo.

❦

When they're angry, Mom's neck gets red and blotchy.
Dad stutters and walks in circles. And flaps his arms.
Robin, 11, Ames, Iowa

Instead of fighting, Dad teases. Like when Mom lost
her credit card, he called her "Dingbat" and
"Airhead." Mom ignores him, but her face gets red.
Lloyd, 15, Austin, Tex.

When they're fighting, Mom talks to the dog
and tells him how mean and terrible my daddy is,
and she pays attention to the dog or to us
kids and ignores Daddy. She doesn't look at
him and treats him like he isn't there.
Jillian, 8, Stamford, Conn.

"Please Don't Kiss Me
at the Bus Stop!"
216

If Dad's mad, he goes in the family room and turns on
the TV real loud so no one can talk to him. Finally,
it's so loud that Mom goes in and turns it off. The TV
goes on and off until they finally have it out.
Savannah, 12, Dallas, Tex.

When they play scrabble, it gets ugly. Sometimes during their games, I pray they'll get divorced. Or kill each other. Anything but play scrabble.

Flora, 13, New York, N.Y.

&

At the mall, Mom told Dad he'd get whiplash watching all the passing skirts. Dad said, "Yeah? When I *stop* looking—that's when you should worry." Before you knew it, they were having a fight.

Jesse, 10, San Jose, Calif.

&

Mom's always late. Dad's always early. By the time we actually leave to go anywhere, they're both going nuts and yelling at each other.

Sherry, 14, Davenport, Iowa

Mom's literary. She analyzes books, discusses their
significance. Dad buys his books by the pound.
He likes fat books that have stealth bombers in them,
and he pretends to analyze them, just to irritate Mom.
Pete, 11, Denver, Colo.

❧

Mom's a Democrat.
Dad swears she does that just to annoy him.
R.J., 13, Dallas, Tex.

❧

Money. They have the same argument every time.
You can almost say the lines along with them.
It's like they're reading a script.
Zach, 11, Reno, Nev.

If they don't like it, they ignore it. They just don't talk about it. This can be a mood, a pimple, a hairstyle. My boyfriend. Inflation. If they don't acknowledge it, it's not there. Or it'll go away.

Kelly, 15, Lexington, Ky.

∞

They say the opposite of what they mean when they're mad. Dad says, "Your logic is beautiful— brilliant. No one can think like you do." What he means is, "Boy, are you dumb!"

Laurie, 18, Wichita, Kans.

∞

They don't fight or yell. They get sarcastic. "Nice work, Honey," means, "Boy, you really screwed up." Or they laugh at you, "A monkey could have written this term paper, Dear."

Lanie, 15, Los Angeles, Calif.

I'm what they fight about. Mom'll say,
"Put your hair up."
Dad'll go, "Her hair looks fine." And off they go.
Or Dad'll say, "Be home by ten."
Mom'll say, "I told her eleven." And off they go.
One'll say, "Did you do your homework?"
The other one'll say, "I told her she could do it
tomorrow." And off they go. It's like, if I weren't
there, what would they fight about?

Margo, 14, Decatur, Ill.

%

Whenever I tell them why I'm mad,
they say I've got a big mouth or I'm spoiled.
But if I don't tell them and just keep it to myself,
they scold me for not talking to them.

Libby, 13, Detroit, Mich.

If I lie because I don't want to get in trouble,
they go on about how much they trust me.
"If you say you didn't do it, we know you didn't do it."
I guess they want me to figure out that it'd be better
if I just tell the truth and get in trouble.
Peggy, 9, Medford, N.J.

⌘

My parents don't take my stuff seriously.
To them, whatever bothers kids is petty or
unimportant. If I tell them what's bothering me,
they'll say, "I hope that's the worst problem
you ever have." Or, "You don't know
how good you have it, kid."
Mace, 12, Providence, R.I.

If I complain about anything, they tease me.
"Poor you. If you only had parents who loved you,
your life would be so much better." Forget it.
Ruth, 10, Portland, Maine

❧

When I'm upset my mom'll bug me till I talk to her
about it. Then she'll say something like, "Well, don't
worry. If it's meant to be, it's meant to be." Or, "No use
crying over spilt milk." Something really helpful.
Tonika, 12, Los Angeles, Calif.

❧

When they're mad, they call me "Harold Finley
Chambers." The rest of the time, I'm Hank.
Hank, 9, Madison, Wis.

❧

My parents are never mad. They're "disappointed."
Eva, 10, Utica, N.Y.

When my mom's mad, she says I'm just like my father.
When my dad's mad, he says I'm just like my mother.

Pete, 8, Springfield, Ill.

⁂

Any time I'm mad at my parents, I'm being "rude."
What am I supposed to do when I'm pissed off,
smile and tell them they're cool?

Arnie, 13, Fresno, Calif.

⁂

I get yelled at for whining. I get yelled at for yelling.
I get yelled at for not talking at all. They say
they want me to talk to them about how I feel,
but when I do, they get mad about the tone of my
voice. They listen to how I'm saying something,
not to what I'm trying to say.

Darlene, 16, Saginaw, Mich.

The way they see things, they're always right.
I'm always wrong. It's that simple. There's no use
arguing or discussing anything.

Tony, 17, Ocean City, N.J.

Okay, an argument's over. But my mom will go on,
repeating her points and the issues again and again,
in case I didn't get her points the first 437 times.

Nick, 16, Duluth, Minn.

Mom never raises her voice. Even when she's furious,
she's very demure and controlled. She sits very straight
and still and curses like you can't believe.

Dave, 15, Austin, Tex.

Dad yells when I can't find my shoes. "Get your shoes on and get in the car!" I can't help it if they're lost.

Beccy, 7, Bridgeport, Conn.

If my brother bugs me, Mom gets sarcastic and tells me to, like, knock him to the ground and sit on him until he begs for mercy. "Whatever you do," she says, "*don't* talk it out. *Anybody* can do *that*. If a kid annoys you, tear his ears off. Be different." She makes you laugh, so you're not so mad.

Keith, 9, Charlotte, N.C.

"Boys," they shout, "Clean up this mess!" If I tell them my brother made the mess, they get angrier because I'm tattling. They don't care who did it. They admit this, too. They say, "It doesn't matter who did it, just clean it up!"

Matt, 12, Portland, Oreg.

They always blame me for what my little brother does.
Zach, 10, Gladwyne, Pa.

They always side with my little sister. If I even call
her a name, like 'No Brain,' I get punished, sent to my
room, no TV for a month, something like that. But she
never gets in trouble. Even if she hits me really hard,
kicks me, and makes my leg black and blue, it's no
big deal. They'll offer her a snack, get her anything
she wants. A CD, a new TV. A pony.
Rachel, 11, Wilmington, Del.

I always have to do more than my share. My sister
never has to do anything. In fact, I get yelled at
if she doesn't do her share. "Help each other,"
they'll say. "Just get it done!"
Jacquie, 10, Laurel, Miss.

If someone calls and doesn't leave a message, it's my fault. It's like a crime. My dad's like, "Well, who *was* it? A man or a woman? Did it sound like a business call? Did it sound important? Why didn't you get a name?" He goes nuts.

James, 13, Cleveland, Ohio

∽

There are four kids in our family. If one acts up, all four get punished. If we're at a swimming pool and my brothers splash too much, the rest of us have to leave, too. If my brothers fight, we all get sent to our rooms.

Lizzie, 8, San Jose, Calif.

∽

When she's in a bad mood, Mom'll turn to me and shout, "Your hair's dirty and you smell like the dog. Go take a shower!"

Leilah, 9, Tucson, Ariz.

My mom's like half my size. Tiny. But when she's mad, she comes after me, threatens to tan my hide. She's seriously scary.

Ronald, 14, St. Paul, Minn.

Mom gets so mad that she snarls.
Eric, 10, Pittsburgh, Pa.

My mother could burn the house down
with her eyes. If she's looking at you, your
skin gets hot and starts to melt.
Craig, 13, Fargo, N.Dak.

Sometimes Dad'll say, "Okay. Let's vote on it."
But he and Mom get two votes, and if there's a tie,
he gets to break it. If you complain that this
is unfair, he says, "You should be glad to get any
votes at all. You're just a kid."
Arlene, 7, Green Bay, Wis.

If you argue with my dad, he says, "This is my house.
I get things my way. This is *not* a democracy."

Kelly, 7, Stamford, Conn.

My dad doesn't listen; when he's mad, he just yells.
If my mom tells him not to yell until he's listened,
he gets mad at her for taking my side.

Sophie, 11, Phoenix, Ariz.

Every time I get in trouble, one of them says,
"We ought to give that kid back to the Gypsies.
Get our money back." The other one says,
"They wouldn't take him." Every time.

Bryan, 8, Silver Springs, Md.

My mother was in labor for thirty-six hours with me.
She still hasn't forgiven me for this.
Whenever she's mad, she says, "Don't give me a hard
time; I pushed and sweated for thirty-six hours
to bring you into this world."

Steve, 12, Stamford, Conn.

❧

If you get mad at my dad, his feelings get hurt.
He sulks. You feel awful.

Stephanie, 11, Atlanta, Ga.

❧

My dad gets mad at machines. Tools. Things he
has to fix. He'll drop a screw or a nut under the porch,
or he'll measure something wrong, and he'll storm
around the house, stomping his feet. If you talk to
him—if you just say, "Dad?" he'll glare at you and
growl, "What do you want now?!"

Darlene, 11, Sacramento, Calif.

Daddy can't stand it when I cry.
He'll give me what I want, usually.
Whitney, 9, Oakland, Calif.

ॐ

Dad panics when I cry. He hugs me and
does whatever he can to make me stop. But if I drag it
out too long, he gets frustrated. There's a peak time to
stop. Otherwise, he'll say, "Okay, go cry it out.
I'm here when you're finished."
Erica, 13, Tulsa, Okla.

ॐ

They say, "What's wrong?" I say, "Nothing."
They can't accept that. "Not nothing," they say,
"something. What is it?" "Nothing." This can go on
for a while, until I manage to find something to
complain about that satisfies them.
Barbara, 18, Chicago, Ill.

My parents would never admit that they worry
about me. But they buy every book they can
find about adolescent girls. Self-esteem.
Gender-specific issues. Eating disorders.
Janice, 13, Larchmont, N.Y.

❧

My mom doesn't say anything when she's mad.
She blows me a raspberry.
Vanessa, 10, San Diego, Calif.

❧

They are bizarre about accidents. They go, "Why did
you drop that?" Or "Why aren't you more careful?"
Like, Mom? Dad?—it was an *accident*.
Sonia, 12, Cheltenham, Pa.

When I accidentally spill or break something,
Mommy doesn't get mad. She just says,
"Well, I guess I'll have to kill you."

Arielle, 7, Gladwyne, Pa.

&

If I spill something, my dad acts like I did it
on purpose. I get the whole "Be Careful and
Look What You're Doing" speech. There's no
way to stop it. If I say, "I'm sorry," he says,
"Sorry doesn't *change* anything."

Robin, 9, Jenkintown, Pa.

&

There's no pressure from my parents, just as long as I'm
perfect. They say they're happy as long as I do my best.
But "do your best" means that, whatever you do, you
could still potentially do better. So you're never good
enough, and they're never happy.

Brad, 19, Cleveland, Ohio

My mom yells. Over nothing. Like if, right now,
I asked her to take me for ice cream or to let me
have a sleepover, she'd yell about how all I ever think
about is myself and how can I ask for something
when she's so tired out and I didn't even take
the dog for a walk and I'm the most spoiled kid in the
world. But then, she'd hear herself yelling, and
feel guilty and apologize. She's totally predictable.
And it's not bad, because she feels so guilty for
overreacting and yelling that she ends up giving me
whatever it was I wanted in the first place. I'd get a
sleepover and *everyone* would go out for ice cream.

Beth, 11, Fort Wayne, Ind.

&

They have a way of saying, "That's okay," or, "Don't
worry about it," that makes you feel like you've done
the worst thing in the world. That you're just slime.

Margie, 15, Meridian, Miss.

"I'm sorry you feel that way." That's how they end
our arguments. So it's on me that I *feel* some way;
the problem has nothing to do with them.

Caitlyn, 16, Tallahassee, Fla.

❧

When I get mad at them they say, "It's just your age;
you're bound to think we're stupid. All kids your age
think that." They wave me off. It's just my age. So what
I think and how I feel aren't worth beans.

Sarah, 13, Toledo, Ohio

❧

My mom disapproves of me. Always has, always will.
I can't please her. Once, a tall, leggy blonde walked
by us. Ma scowled at me and said,
"Why can't you look like her?"
Now, Mom's five feet tall and just as wide. So I
explained, "I can't look like her, Ma, because I look just
like you." She scowled again and told me I was fresh.

Susan, 20, Tampa, Fla.

Mom worries that I'm not popular enough. I always
have to reassure her. I tell her I'm happy. I'm fine.
I don't need to be with other kids all the time. She
doesn't let up. "Why don't you invite Andrea over?"
"I don't like Andrea, Mom."
"Why? She seems like a sweet girl."
"She's boring."
"Well, how about Christine?"
"Christine's a creep."
"Really? Her mother's awfully nice. How
about Natalie?"
Rita, 11, St. Louis, Mo.

❧

They analyze everything. "Why did you *really* do that?
Were you expressing hostility when you turned on the
TV while your sister was studying? Or when you ate
the last cookie without asking?" Nothing's just what
it is. For my parents, there's always some hidden
meaning. And we need to discuss it.
Hal, 13, New York, N.Y.

If my mom and I disagree, she'll say anything to get her way. She'll tell me I'm too old or too young. She'll say I should ask her later or that I shouldn't wait till the last minute to ask her. She says, "Your friend John would never do that." Or, "I don't care *what* John does— you're not John." She'll say anything, be completely inconsistent, if it works to her advantage.

Evan, 12, Washington, D.C.

✿

They lie to make things seem okay, or to make me feel good. They tell me I look lovely when I'm overweight and have a big pimple on my nose. They say they like my outfit when I'm dressed like a dweeb.

Myra, 11, Raleigh, N.C.

✿

Instead of arguing, they try to pay you off. They think money can buy anything. Dad said, "Quit going out with that guy Sal and I'll make your car payment."

Lynda, 18, Wilkes-Barre, Pa.

When they're mad, you hear, "As long as you live
in my house, under my roof . . ." Or, "As long
as I pay the bills and you eat my food . . ." They never
give in. There's no chance of reasoning with them;
things are their way or no way at all.
Sondra, 17, Norwich, Conn.

❧

"Just wait and see what I leave you in the will."
That's what Mom says when she's mad
but doesn't feel like arguing.
Arnie, 12, Rockford, Ill.

❧

They get real mad when I can't find the hamster.
Stephanie, 6, Indianapolis, Ind.

My parents even argue about death. My dad'll say,
"I don't want to be buried near your parents. I want to
be cremated and scattered at sea."
Mom'll get upset. "No way. You've got to be next to
me." Dad'll say, "Have your ashes scattered along
with mine." Mom'll snap, "No way. The kids'll
have no place to visit us."
Dad'll turn to us and say, "Hey, kids? What do
you think? Would you rather go to the
beach or a cemetery?"
Melanie, 13, Portland, Oreg.

Our bird died. Dad flushed it. No funeral. Nothing
was ever said about it. One day there was a bird.
The next day there wasn't. The cage wasn't
even there. Nobody said a word about it.
Like, bird? What bird?
Ben, 9, Denver, Colo.

When my goldfish died, they had a funeral. They read poems. Like it was a big deal. Actually, I was glad the thing died. No bowl to clean anymore.

Josh, 8, Topeka, Kans.

When Grandma died, they didn't let us go to the funeral. They said we were still kids and they didn't want us to be upset. As if we wouldn't be anyway.

Ellie, 9, Detroit, Mich.

The piano teacher died. They thought I'd be too upset to play the piano ever again. I'm sorry she died. But, look, they'd never have let me drop piano if she'd lived.

Hollis, 11, Wilmette, Ill.

My grandfather died last fall and my parents won't
stop talking about it. How it affects us. Do we
have dreams about him? Are we afraid of somebody
else dying? Do we believe in Heaven?

Germaine, 10, Philadelphia, Pa.

∽

People don't die. They "go to Florida." If Mom
says someone's in Florida, you know they're dead.
Unless, well, sometimes, they're in Florida.

Maggie, 10, Brentwood, Calif.

∽

Mom burns candles for all the dead people she knows.
There's always candles burning in the living room.

Carl, 9, Brooklyn, N.Y.

Our cat got run over by a car, but my mom insists
she ran away. I know the cat's dead. The whole
neighborhood knows. But Mom insists that Paws
just ran off and got a new home somewhere.
Yeah, Mom. It's called Heaven.

Will, 14, Bethesda, Md.

❧

Mom worries. She waits for disasters. If Dad doesn't
call and comes home late, she's frantic. She's sure he's
been in a car accident. But she doesn't want him to
know she was worried, so she acts *real normal* when he
comes in. Every time. Meantime, she's called every hos-
pital, seeing if he's been admitted.

Celia, 10, Ft. Worth, Tex.

It doesn't matter what they do or how obnoxious they are. If I get mad at my sisters, Mom says, "One day, you girls will be alone. Dad and I won't be here to work things out. You'll be the only blood relatives you have. So don't fight, unless you're on the same side." So, bottom line, they can do anything, and I'm not supposed to get mad.

Kendra, 10, Rochester, N.Y.

⁓

Mom's always reminding us that, someday, she's going to die. "Whatever happens, don't put me on life support." She'll see an old lady with a walker, and she'll say, "When I'm like that, shoot me." She also says, "Don't waste money on a cemetery plot. Just cremate me. Spread my ashes to the wind. Dust to dust."

Shelley, 19, Binghamton, N.Y.

"Please Don't Kiss Me
at the Bus Stop!"
244

My Parents, Myself

From the moment of birth, children begin the process of separating from their parents. As they mature, they display increasing independence, making their own decisions, asserting their authority, discovering their own identities. Gradually, kids choose their own wardrobes, companions, and activities; take charge of their own relationships and responsibilities; go for their own goals; and make their own mistakes. Struggling, stumbling, or storming through the phases and stages of growing up, they wrestle with mixed, uncertain feelings—not only their own, but also their parents'.

"My parents tell me, 'Just be yourself,'" says Raymond, fourteen. "Okay. So, what does *that* mean? I

245

mean, who else *could* I be? Or, like, who do they think I *should* be that I'm not?"

Many young people insist that they want their parents to let go, not cling, not nag, and not interfere. Others admit that they prefer balance to abandonment, flexible bonds rather than boundless freedom. Either way, kids want parents to see the differences between umbilical cords and emotional ties, apron strings and safety nets. Young children need security as they step out into the world, and, even as they seek freedom, most older kids need the solid ground of a place to come home to, if only to do laundry and remember why they've left.

❧

They never let me do things myself. They're afraid I'll mess up. They say, "Here, let me help you." "Here, let me pour that for you." Or, "Here, I'll cut that for you." They chase me around the kitchen, taking stuff from me.

Meredith, 7, Skokie, Ill.

They say I should make my own decisions, so they never just come out and warn me that I'm about to make a mistake. They never say, "Are you nuts? You'd be crazy to do that!" But later, after I've goofed up big-time, they say, "We *knew* that would happen. We could have told you so!"

Derek, 16, Casper, Wyo.

❧

My parents tell me to make up my own mind, but then they don't like my decision. They frown. They sigh. They ask, "Are you *sure*?" They pause, shake their heads, and say, "Well, if you *really, truly* think that's the right choice . . ."

Monica, 13, Boise, Idaho

❧

When they don't agree with my opinions, they say, "Oh, grow up!" As if anybody who isn't a complete *infant* would see things their way.

Dottie, 15, Santa Fe, N.Mex.

They ask me something when they already
know the answer. "What time did you come home last
night?" I say, "About twelve." They say, "It was
twelve-twenty, actually."
If I say, "Why'd you ask me if you knew?" they say,
"We wanted to hear it from you." Everything's got
layers; nothing's simple. It's not only about what time
I came home, it's about whether or not I'm going to tell
the truth about it. A booby trap.

Evelyn, 18, Baltimore, Md.

Mom meets me at the bus stop after school.
She won't let me walk two blocks home alone.

Latisha, 8, Skokie, Ill.

They correct me. They can't stand it if I start a sentence
with "Well," or "Like." They hate the word "stuff."
Like they don't let me say stuff the way I want to.

Leslie, 11, Decatur, Ill.

They make plans for me without even talking to me
about them first. Kids come over that I don't want
to see. I get signed up for a camp I don't want to go to.
They tell me, "Get ready, you're late." Late for what?
I have no plans—that I *know* of.
Rachel, 9, San Francisco, Calif.

❧

If I don't want to do what they want to do, like go
out to eat with Aunt Beulah, or play bingo at the fire
station, or whatever, they tell me I'm so negative,
or that I'm always ruining the fun. They don't get
it that I just don't want to do whatever it is.
They have to give me a whole guilt trip.
Callie, 14, Miller, Ind.

❧

Before I leave the house to go anywhere,
my mom yells, "Nick! Go to the bathroom."
Nicholas, 14, Shreveport, La.

It's like they think my friends and I are idiots.
When we go anywhere they say, "Remember—don't get
in a car with anyone who's been drinking or taking
drugs. Call and we'll pick you up. Do you
have a quarter for a phone call?"
Gary, 15, St. Louis, Mo.

⤴

Can I get my own phone? No. Can I get my own TV?
No. Can I get my own car? No. Can I use theirs? No.
Paula, 16, Tulsa, Okla.

⤴

I'm going to a party or a Bar Mitzvah and Dad says, "I'll
come in with you." Then he says to the kid's parents,
"You'll be here all night, right? You'll take care of my
Dena, right?" Then, as if that's not bad enough, he yells,
"BYE, DENA. I'M LEAVING NOW. BE GOOD!"
Dena, 13, Highland Park, Ill.

"Please Don't Kiss Me
at the Bus Stop!"
250

Dad's teaching me to drive. He yells over nothing,
like if I don't hit the brake the *second* he says to.
He screams, "Brake!" and grabs the dashboard.
I mean, it's not like I've *hit* anything.
Cooper, 15, Detroit, Mich.

Dad won't let me use the car. I've had my license for
four months, but he won't let me drive.
Diego, 16, Pittsburgh, Pa.

If I want to stay up and read or rearrange
my bookshelf or closet, forget it. Bedtime is bedtime,
whether I'm tired or not. They think they
should decide when I go to sleep.
Rachel, 11, Dallas, Tex.

My Parents,
Myself

251

Mom goes with me everywhere. She waits at Little League, soccer, swimming. She volunteers at school. She teaches at Sunday School. Probably, she'll go with me to college. Maybe I'll be an astronaut.

Keith, 9, Radnor, Pa.

My mom talks to my friends. I mean, she *talks* to them,
like she asks them about movies, their parents,
boys. She can't just let them alone. Or say, "Hi,
how's it going?" and keep moving.

Lauren, 15, Jackson, Miss.

They say I can get a dog when I'm old enough to take
care of it myself. Probably that means I can get a
dog when I move into my own house.

Nadya, 8, Amherst, Mass.

They interrupt me. It doesn't matter if I'm reading,
studying, talking on the phone—they just interrupt.
About stupid stuff—did you clean your room? Do you
know where your shoes are? Whatever—but, trust me,
even if it's important, *I* can't ever interrupt *them*.

Baxter, 9, Washington, D.C.

My mom's so out there that there's nothing left
for me to do. Nothing I do could shock her. She's
used drugs, spiked her hair, dyed it green; she has about
thirty ear holes, a butterfly tattoo. She's done all the
diets, lifestyles, all the religions. She had me
before she married my father. She's been divorced
three times. I've told her that the only way
I can rebel against a mother like her is to
become a right-wing conservative.

Jason, 13, New York, N.Y.

❦

I dyed a magenta stripe in my hair and my
parents didn't notice. Or they pretended not to.
See, they try not to oppose me. They're
afraid that if they give me a hard time,
I'll give them a harder one.

Dixie, 16, Arlington, Va.

If I have the slightest problem with a kid or a teacher,
my parents run to the school, talk to my
counselor or the principal like it's a major crisis.
They make it a major crisis.

Cody, 11, Seattle, Wash.

&

I get good grades, but that's not enough. I do well in
sports, but that's not enough. They say, "Talent's only 10
percent. The other 90 percent is who you know, dumb
luck, and recognizing opportunities." They tell me to
"get along" and "connect." It's never too early to start.

Rod, 15, Louisville, Ky.

&

I got a haircut a couple weeks ago. You'd think
I had won the Olympics, they were so proud. They
called all the relatives, half the town.

Ed, 18, Norfolk, Conn.

They'll tell me to go get dressed, and when I'm dressed
and ready to go, they'll say, "You're wearing *that?*"
Carla, 14, Elgin, Ill.

I'm ready to go out and Dad says, "Young
lady, have you looked in the mirror? You're
not leaving this house in that!"
Opal, 16, Memphis, Tenn.

Lots of times, I put on a dorky layer of clothes
over my outfits so I don't have to listen to their stuff
about what I'm wearing. When I get where
I'm going, I stick the dorky stuff in a bag and
put it on again when I go home.
Madeline, 14, Savannah, Ga.

My mom puts my clothes out the night before.
She chooses what I wear. No discussions.
Sarah, 11, Gladwyne, Pa.

❧

Mom borrows my clothes. Without even asking.
Nothing of mine is safe.
Dakota, 15, Dallas, Tex.

❧

One of them will look at me and say,
"Your lipstick's awfully dark, isn't it?"
Eileen, 17, Richmond, Va.

❧

I'm ready to go somewhere and Mom makes a face and
says, "Is that what kids are wearing these days?"
Tamara, 14, Darien, Conn.

I got my hair cut real short. My mom said,
"Goodness. What a man-hating thing to do."
Amanda, 18, Somerset, N.J.

When I got my second ear hole, you'd think I'd robbed
a *bank*. Mom told me I was mutilating my body. Lord.
Wait till they find out about the tattoo.
Sydney, 17, Knoxville, Tenn.

My mom's totally paranoid, worrying that I might ever
smoke cigarettes or try pot. Or have sex. Guess what?
Summer, 16, Los Angeles, Calif.

Whenever I come home, they give me the third degree.
I don't know what they want me to tell them. Nothing
happened. We didn't go anywhere, didn't do anything.
But they keep asking. I'm tempted to make stuff up,
"We sold Tim's little sister to some drug dealer guy.
We held up an old lady." Would that satisfy them?

Rick, 15, Pine Bluff, Ark.

If I bring home a guy who's a different race or religion,
they drill me. "How serious are you? How long have
you been involved?" It doesn't matter if a guy is a serial
killer, a bum, or a drug addict—all they care about
is that he's of my race and religion.

Latisha, 19, Atlanta, Ga.

I had a gay friend over. My parents figured that if I
have a gay friend, I must be gay, too. The rest of the
week, they were freaked. All they could do was hint,
ask if there was anything I wanted to talk about.
Mel, 18, Detroit, Mich.

How other people met their fiancés is all my mom talks
about. "Did you know that Suzi met her husband at the
dentist?" Implying what? That I should hang out at
dentists' offices? "Kathy met her fiancé on a flight to
Brazil." So, what? I should go to Brazil?
Lynda, 20, Tacoma, Wash.

I introduced this guy I was going out with to
my mom. The next day, she said—real casually—
"You know, Maxine, rich guys need loving
just as much as poor ones."
Maxine, 19, Fort Wayne, Ind.

Every time I have a date, my mom disapproves. She says stuff like, "Would it hurt you, just once, to go out with someone from your own planet?"

Susan, 19, Boston, Mass.

Mom tells me about other people's successes all the time. Remember Suzy So-and-so? She's got a job in France. Sara Such-and-such married a zillionaire. Sophie So-and-such is going to Harvard. What she's *really* saying, of course, is, "And you? What's there to say about *you*? Nothing! Nothing! Nothing!"

Naomi, 20, Brooklyn, N.Y.

Mom can't sleep unless everyone's in bed. She waits up. If I stay out late with friends, I have to hear how exhausted she is the next day.

Sondra, 17, Louisville, Ky.

Dad interviews my dates. He "talks" to them for
a while. I don't even want to go out by the time he's
finished. After I come home, he gives me his "insights,"
asks if I'm "serious" about the guy. As if I can be
serious about anybody when I'm seventeen years old.

Kendra, 17, Des Moines, Iowa

∝

My dad mimics the guys I go out with.
He does impressions. Imitates how they walk.

Letitia, 17, Dover, Del.

∝

Dad waits up for me when I go out at night.
"To kiss me goodnight."

Shannon, 16, Darien, Conn.

Dad treats my boyfriends like criminals. He looks
them over, head to toe, like he's going to challenge
them to a gunfight. Or meet them out back.

Diane, 15, Honolulu, Hawaii

☙

Whenever I'm leaving on a date, Dad kisses me
and says, "Remember, we trust you."

Amelia, 15, Evanston, Ill.

☙

Dad says, "Don't think you can do or think of doing
anything we haven't done or thought of doing." Sounds
like a dare to me. Well, okay, Dad—you're on.

John, 16, Ft. Worth, Tex.

They're old fashioned. I have to be home by nine o'clock. I can't date until I'm sixteen, and even then they say they'll want to talk about it with the boy's parents. They say I should take a lesson from my cousin Mindy who didn't date until she was twenty, and then she married the first boy who took her out.

Donna, 13, Winston-Salem, N.C.

❧

If I bring a boyfriend home after a date, my mom suddenly has the urge to do laundry or vacuum. At midnight.

Maria, 16, Kalamazoo, Mich.

❧

I was on a date, at the movies. Mom and Dad just happened to go to the same show. "Uh. Hi, Mom. Hi, Dad." They wanted to double date, go for pizza after.

Nora, 16, Evanston, Ill.

My date shows up, and Dad says,
"So, you been driving long? Ever get a ticket?"
Claire, 16, Park Ridge, Ill.

❧

When they come to pick me up, Dad tells my dates,
"Take good care of my little girl."
Diane, 15, Portland, Oreg.

❧

Mom chitchats with my dates as if they're there to see
her. Then she takes me in the kitchen and says, "He's
cute." Like, Mom, can you say it any louder?
Debra, 15, Miami, Fla.

❧

If I'm, like, five minutes late, I'm grounded.
Phil, 13, Boulder, Colo.

They bought me a portable phone, and they call me if I'm ten minutes late. Or to tell me to run an errand for them, or to do some chore when I get home.

Tanya, 17, Buffalo, N.Y.

✍

I'm on the phone, in the middle of a major fight with my boyfriend, and they expect me to just suddenly hang up and come downstairs because it's time for dinner. Like nothing should get in the way of food.

Lily, 15, Denver, Colo.

✍

Mom keeps track of my snacks. It's like she has a list of my intake or something. "You just ate three pretzels. Why are you taking cereal?"

Whitney, 13, Merion, Pa.

They're always on me about food. "You're so skinny—have a piece of chicken?" If I don't take it, they offer me sandwiches, donuts, cake, strudel, cheese, whatever's in the house.
Karen, 14, New York, N.Y.

❧

We have all these food issues. Mom wants me to fill up with meat and potatoes. She's afraid I'm anorexic because I like yogurt.
Susanna, 15, Peoria, Ill.

❧

"You're too thin—eat something." I mean, why can't my parents let me decide whether or not I'm hungry?
Dana, 13, Syracuse, N.Y.

Mom wants me to cook with her. Learn Grandma's
recipes for pot roast, chopped liver, duckling.
Never mind that I'm a vegetarian.

Patty, 14, Cleveland, Ohio

❧

"That's enough syrup!" "Not so much cake!"
"You'll get pimples from all that chocolate!" I hear
these things even when my mom isn't there,
because she's said it so much.

Opal, 16, Lansdale, Pa.

❧

To Mom, I'll always be a little boy. I came home
from college for Thanksgiving break and was
going out with some friends. Mom yelled,
"Be home by ten!" She calls me at the dorm on
cold days to remind me to wear a scarf.

Bob, 19, Cherry Hill, N.J.

When I was away at camp, Mom wrote me
every day. She reminded me to brush my teeth and
wash my hair. She wrote that she was upset that
I hadn't written. Then she wrote that she was
upset that I'd only written once.

Lottie, 12, Scarsdale, N.Y.

❧

They expected me to come home from camp and be
the same as before. I'd just spent two months
without having to listen to them. I'd made my own
rules and decisions. Now it's back to, "Take a shower.
Clear the table. Go to bed."

Mike, 13, Syracuse, N.Y.

❧

They washed my sleeping bag.
Now it doesn't smell like camp anymore.

Evie, 12, Atlanta, Ga.

I was invited on a sleepover, and my mother sent the bear I used to sleep with in my sleeping bag. She wrote a note: "In case you need this. And here are good-night kisses: XXXXXXXXXXXX."

Austin, 8, Cincinnati, Ohio

❧

They want me to walk the neighbors' dogs, sell lemonade. Start a business. Get a job.

Brent, 8, St. Louis, Mo.

❧

I babysat for the neighbors. Mom called three times. On the hour. To see how I was doing.

Elise, 12, Newark, Del.

❧

They don't think we should see PG-13 movies. We'll get corrupted by Hollywood or something.

Dick, 11, Phoenix, Ariz.

My parents won't let me go to the movies
alone with my friends. One goes along and sits
in the back row. "Just in case."

Kendra, 9, Wilmington, Del.

They tell me how to spend my allowance money.
Whatever I want to buy is a waste.
Dexter, 10, Philadelphia, Pa.

❧

Every time I get a dime, they tell me to put it in
savings. "Invest your money." They won't let me
decide how to handle my own funds.
Jeremy, 11, Swarthmore, Pa.

❧

They talk as if your age is what you should do. "You're
ten years old—finish your math." "You're ten years
old—put your bike in the garage." "For gosh sakes,
you're ten years old—wipe the ketchup off your
mouth." "I'm surprised at you!—you're ten years old!"
Laura, 10, Terre Haute, Ind.

My younger sister gets to do all kinds of things
at ten that I wasn't allowed to till I was fifteen.
She has her own phone. She can stay up to watch TV,
pick the shows she watches. She can shop
for her own clothes. She has complete freedom.
This is so unfair; it was *not* like that for me. I couldn't
breathe without their permission.

Dawn, 16, Casper, Wyo.

❧

They like my friends to come to my house,
not me to go to my friends', so they can supervise.
When I go to friends' houses, they say, "If you
have an 'uh-oh feeling,' listen to it, and come home."
When I get home, they ask what we did, who was
there. If the parents own guns.

Marybeth, 9, Tuscaloosa, Ala.

They criticize everything. "How can you have the radio on while you do homework? How can you sleep with all those pillows? How can you eat that? How can you wear that? How can you say that?" Whatever.

Ellen, 13, Eureka, Nev.

❧

They check my homework, read my papers.
They stand behind me and read over my shoulder.
Like I can't do my own work?

Veronica, 13, Yonkers, N.Y.

❧

Dad doesn't like me to play computer games. He says it's antisocial. But guess who bought the computer?

Vince, 14, Orlando, Fla.

I'm not allowed to go across the street
without a parent.
Alexis, 7, Wayne, Pa.

When they go out, they make me stay
with a babysitter. It's humiliating.
Ken, 9, Fort Worth, Tex.

They let my brother babysit for me.
I'd be safer with Godzilla.
Ted, 8, New Haven, Conn.

Mom wants me to do my own laundry,
but she complains if I don't do it her way. "You
can't wash that in hot water! Don't put in
so much bleach! No! Don't fold it like *that*!"
Pam, 14, Manchester, N.H.

Now that I have a job, they charge me for
my share of the food. Mom asked me for two
dollars for the knockwurst I ate.
Bruce, 17, Boise, Idaho

When I left for college, Mom gave me a list of all the
relatives' addresses, phone numbers, and birthdays.
Bob, 20, Wynnewood, Pa.

If I use the car, I'm expected to fill the gas tank.
Never mind it was on empty when I took it out.
Lloyd, 17, Southfield, Mich.

⚜

Dad says he doesn't mind if I use the car.
But he goes nuts that the seat's adjusted for my
size or that the car radio's on my station.
Stacey, 17, Baton Rouge, La.

⚜

Dad doesn't think I can manage money on my own.
He thinks I need his help. Whenever I go out,
he slips a twenty in my pocket and says, "Here.
Always take a kicker."
Hank, 18, Houston, Tex.

My dad always says, "Before you do something, think
of the consequences. Ask yourself, 'If I do this,
then what will happen?'" Now I'm a camp counselor,
and I heard myself tell my campers, "Before
you do something, consider the consequences. Ask
yourselves..." And I thought, "Oh, no. This is scary."

Mike, 17, Utica, N.Y.

∞

Dad says, "You know, I'm not as dumb as you think.
When you have your own kids, suddenly I'll seem very
smart." Mom says, "Wait till *you* have kids. What goes
around comes around. The last laugh'll be mine."

Gussie, 15, Shreveport, La.